HERBS

SPHERE COLOUR PLANT GUIDES
HERBS

SPHERE BOOKS LIMITED
30-32 Gray's Inn Road, London WCIX 8JL

CONTENTS

Production: Inmerc BV, Wormer, Holland, and Mercurius UK Ltd.,
Northgate House, Plough Rd, Gt. Bentley, Colchester, Essex.
Compilation: Rob van Maanen.
Text: Tony Loynes.
Photography: Joop Valk, Harry Smith, Bob van der Lans,
Hollington Nurseries.
Photo cover: Harry Smith.
Layout: Loek de Leeuw.
Typesetting: RCO/Telezet BV, Velp.
Printing: BV Kunstdrukkerij Mercurius-Wormerveer, Holland.
This edition published by Sphere Books Ltd., London 1984.
Reprinted 1985.
© 1984 Mercbook International Ltd., Guernsey.

INTRODUCTION

Few plants you will ever grow are capable of providing the sheer pleasure and versatility of the herb.

For ease of growing and the range of uses to which they can be put herbs are unrivalled. As this book will show they can be used for cooking, preserving, health, colour, aroma and even for beauty.

And for a plant which will give you so many rewards the herb is a generally undemanding one because it is not especially fussy, in most cases, about soil types or treatment....though, as with all plants, the better the care the better the results. Until fairly recently the use of herbs in most homes was limited. Mint was commonly used in mint sauce for eating with lamb, sage and thyme were known largely for their use in stuffing the chicken or turkey and parsley and chives were, perhaps, also found growing outside the kitchen door.

A greater awareness of the incredible versatility of herbs has resulted in the appearance of the ubiquitous herb rack in a vast number of homes.

But how much are herbs - fresh and dried - used? Most of us are still only exploiting a small part of the potential of herbs and this book aims to give some idea of the extraordinary range of uses of garden herbs.

The central section of colour photographs gives a comprehensive guide to 106 herbs with descriptions, advice on cultivation and uses. Other chapters in this book will tell you about the remarkable history of herbs, advise on creating your own herb garden and explain in more detail the uses to which they can be put. It is no coincidence that the medical world is returning more and more to herbs for an answer to many ailments. People are growing increasingly suspicious of the effects upon their bodies of drugs and the appeal of "natural" remedies has consequently grown. Equally, the lure of nature's own produce for cosmetics has grown enormously of late. Hardly a face-care, perfume or hair treatment product is without herbal ingredients. The joy of herbs, however, can be far more simple. The rich, heady smell of rosemary wafting up from a garden plant as you brush it, the magnificent burst of colour from the marigold and the mouth-watering pleasure that the addition of tarragon gives to chicken can be enjoyed by all regardless of the size of garden or the relative skills of the gardener.

A herb, or herbaceous plant, is defined in most dictionaries as "a plant with no woody stem above the ground". But for the purposes of this book that definition is too limiting and here a herb becomes that most flexible of plants - one which has culinary, cosmetic or medical applications, amongst which we find annuals and perennials of all sorts.

Almost as long as man has existed he has eaten and used herbs. Over the years he learned what was safe to eat, what might be used in other ways and what was poisonous.

This process of trial and error, often harmful to the lives of those involved, has built up a collective wisdom which is available to all of us and it would be a great shame if we did not use at least some of it.

Many herbs now used for cooking were originally used in medicine and magic and the powers of some, often hallucinogenic, account for one or two of the more fantastic myths and legends also passed down to us.

Archeological evidence from prehistoric lake sites in Switzerland shows the use of seasonings like poppy and caraway seed but the first documentary evidence available around 2000BC shows the use of far more. Accounts from the Chinese record the use of herbs like anise, saffron, cumin, flag and tarragon and Babylonian records from the same period list medicinal uses of bay tree, thyme, coriander and caraway.

In many ways it would have been remarkable if the uses of these herbs had not been discovered and exploited since they were growing there, plentifully, where the Chinese, the Babylonians and other ancient peoples found them. What remained was the sometimes dangerous process of experimentation to learn how best to use what nature had so bountifully provided.

Once the early races learned how to use herbs the word spread rapidly. Kings and conquerors, sea-faring nations and the great explorers all started removing herbs from their natural soil and taking them all over the globe trying, and in many cases succeeding, to plant them in their home countries.

But it wasn't just the Chinese and the Babylonian peoples who discovered herbs. The Bible tells us that the Hebrews had long used many herbs native to the Middle East though, in the early days, Hebrew religion prevented them from interfering with the purpose of God by trying to heal themselves.

The Romans are said to have brought over 200 varieties of herbs to Britain to be used both in cooking and medicine and this legacy remains today. In fact one Roman scholar, writing during the reign of Tiberius, recommended that food be seasoned with garlic, onion, chives, dill, cumin, fennel, coriander, parsley, saffron, ginger, juniper, bay leaf, pepper, rue, tarragon, mustard, myrtle, sage, savory and thyme. It is not recorded whether all were to be used at the same time, nor what the man died from!

After these early discoveries the fame and reputation of herbs spread worldwide by word of mouth, writings and through the transport of the herbs themselves. The great majority of those found useful survive today. Of the nine sacred herbs of the Anglo-Saxons - mugwort, plantain, watercress, chamomile, nettle, crab apple, chervil, fennel and atterlothe, only the obscure latter is no longer in use. It is fair to assume, however, that ''elf-shot'' for which some were used, is no longer a major problem.

It was obviously quite natural that, since they were so useful to man, herbs should soon find an established place on his property and with the establishment of the Christian church in Britain this is what happened. Herbs left by the Romans were absorbed into monastery gardens and properly cultivated by the monks for their healing properties. While the more mystical herbal uses were still flourishing outside, the monasteries became the centre for the herbal healing methods that developed rapidly in the Middle Ages.

From this period until the 18th century herbs were used almost exclusively for their healing properties. Writers like John Gerard, apothecary to James 1 in 1597, published herbals cataloguing plants and their medicinal uses.

In 1652 Nicholas Culpepper proclaimed various astrological theories in a herbal which announced that every plant had a ''signature'' in that its appearance resembled the part of the body it treated or the cause of the malady. Thus the leaves of pulmonaria resembled the lung therefore they were used to treat it. The theory gained great support for a while.

But in the 18th century, as science developed and superstition retreated, the use of medicinal herbs went into decline and plant remedies were soon considered unfashionable....an attitude which prevailed until the last twenty years or so.

From the middle of the 18th century a new fashion developed, however. Herbs started to be brought into the kitchen garden and in Betty Langley's New Principles of Gardening, published in 1728, a "gentleman's" garden was considered poor unless it had some 50 herbs spread abundantly over 3 acres.

English cookbooks started to appear and while the expensive herb industry fell into decline the herb started to enjoy a grand revival in culinary usage.

In the last twenty years, however, herbs have really come into their own and at long last are being enjoyed for the full range of their uses. Bulk processing of modern foods, the addition of preservatives, the growing suspicion of the effects of drug doses and the appeal of natural products in cosmetics - all have most recently contributed towards a renaissance for the herb.

It's a sobering but at the same time inspiring thought that it has taken all this time for the herb to be truly appreciated.

HERBS IN THE GARDEN

Designing the herb garden

In many ways a herb garden requires more care in the planning than it does at any time afterwards. You don't need to be a horticultural genius to plant and maintain a marvellous herb garden but if it is to serve you properly then it should be planned with great care.

Traditionally herb gardens have been placed near the kitchen since this cut down on the travel to and fro' and it may well be that, all things considered, this is where you plant yours. But before you settle on this, merely to save a change of shoes in the winter, consider all the other factors. A herb garden does not simply produce culinary leaves and seeds. Its benefits come also from the marvellous aroma, splashes of colour and shape. The smell rendered by certain herbs may make you want to plant them near or alongside a path so that humans or animals brushing up against them better release the aroma. The colour of your herb plants may mean you want to place them somewhere that can be seen from the kitchen window rather than underneath it. Sight and smell, then, ought to be considered.

But what about the plants themselves? They, too, would want their needs considered. Most herbs need as much sunshine as possible during their growing season since many come from warmer climes. While they will grow happily over here an effort should be made to plant them in conditions which come as close as possible to those in their native environment. The closer you get the greater will be your rewards both in flavour and fragrance. Herbs generally also need to be protected from the wind so try and site them near a wall, garden shed or in some other sheltered spot.

Study the individual listings for herbs in our central section and you will find all their requirements. This will enable you to know just how to get the best from your herbs.

Drainage is also a very important factor. Few herbs enjoy damp, soggy conditions and those that do might well suit another spot in your garden. It is as well to bear in mind that you need not plant all your herbs in a herb garden. Some may find they enjoy life better somewhere else and you may have a particular reason for siting them elsewhere. A highly-scented herb, for instance, might be placed near a patio to give you the full benefits in warm summer nights.

Before choosing your site consider also size and access. The details given in our individual herb listings include the height to which your herbs will grow. Clearly it is important to plant tall herbs at the rear of your bed so they do not obscure the rest. Plants which do not grow tall but spread out over the ground also need to be planned in carefully. As to access, again you need to consider what you plant and where because herbs which you will use regularly need to be somewhere handy.

Finally, and here again the information you need is in our individual listings, you will need to consider whether the herbs you are planting are perennial or annual. You may consider, initially, that annuals will be too much trouble. But you would be depriving yourself of a great deal of enjoyment should you do so. Whatever decision you reach it would be best to plant them separately. Plant your perennials in a largish bed with edging plants like chives, thymes, sage, marjoram and parsley to the front and hedge plants like lavender and rosemary to the rear or side.

Clearly, then, there are a lot of things to be considered when starting a herb bed - but all of them important if you are to design a useful, rewarding and enjoyable herb garden for years to come. Why not try and draw a plan of your garden. A visual idea of what you have in mind with the size, scale and plants marked down, should help to resolve all the various different considerations.

Finding forms
When it comes to actually designing the look, shape, size and the visual style of your herb garden it would be as well to seek a compromise between beauty and practicality. Many old herb gardens were designed for their intricate and beautiful arrangements, incorporating mazes, herbal knots and other devices. These take a good deal of time to design, plant and maintain and unless you have a gardener might well prove to be beyond your resources. You could, however, steal a few ideas should you want an attractive lay-out. The symmetry of some of the old designs, for instance, could give your garden visual appeal. So, too, could ideas about the shape of beds.

Most people will, however, aim for the cottage garden style approach and for this there are a number of attractive features that can be considered.

Brick walls with the odd brick removed and filled with soil can provide a marvellous and unusual spot for some special herbs.

So, too, can garden containers like tubs, sinks, buckets and old rainwater butts. If you have a garden seat why not plant around it some sweet-smelling herbs to give you that added pleasure when you sit down. A special chamomile lawn could be laid around the base. Bare yards and patios can be transformed with small beds and pot-grown herbs.

Even if you have the sort of garden capable of accommodating a large herb garden it is unlikely that you would want one. It is best to start small and, as your experience and needs develop so can the size of your herb garden.

A good basic plan would be to start with a square which has two diagonal paths meeting in a stone circle at the middle. This would give you four sections into which you could plan your herbs. Start off with one or two of each variety and remember, you will be walking those paths regularly so make

sure you put down a solid foundation.

If you really don't have much room then why not try building a two, or three-tiered herb garden. Make sure your spot, which will have to be against a wall or across a corner of a wall, is not damp or shaded. See too that only your bricks or concrete touch the wall so as not to transmit damp. Once this is done you can start to build your garden upwards in tiers instead of outwards. This will give you a herb garden capable of growing a significant number of herbs, but in a small area.

Maintenance of the herb garden

For the investment of a small amount of time and effort during the growing season the reward can be great. Looking after your herbs during this time is largely a question of weeding and watering. Weed by hand wherever possible and keep them down with a peat dressing. Black polythene sheeting can also be used and this has the added benefit of keeping the soil warm at the same time.

Water the plants regularly when the weather is dry. At the end of the growing period shrubby perennials will need to be cut back by half that year's growth to keep the bushes healthy and the leaves and flowers that remain should be picked and dried. In the autumn or early spring spread a thin layer of well-balanced fertilizer on the soil and work it in lightly. Use sparingly. The less hardy plants like bay and tarragon will need to be potted and brought inside or, at the very least, given a good wrap-up in straw to keep out the cold.

Preparation

The soil for your herb garden will need a certain amount of preparation. Though most herbs will grow in any soil, drainage is important and, if necessary, you may have to build a soakaway if you are determined to have your herb garden in a spot with poor drainage.

To find out how good your drainage is, dig a hole about three feet deep and leave it for a few days. If water collects in the hole then drainage is not good and remedial action may need to be taken. To build a soakaway is simple enough. Dig a hole 1m (3 feet) deep and 60 cm (2ft) square and fill with clinker or broken brick rubble and stones to within 30 cm (1ft) of the top and then replace your top soil.

Your site will need to have been well dug in September or October and then dressed and given an application of lime, if the soil needs it. Preparing it at this time of the year means that the summer warmth in the soil is still enough to help de-compose the turned-in material. The winter frosts that follow will break-up the soil improving both the texture and drainage and allowing the air to get right in. Allow the soil to stand all winter and in the spring dig in compost or manure.

Dressing

For the best results, and in order to improve your soil, it is important to add the dressing your soil needs. Animal manure or compost are the commonest dressing available and perhaps the best is really well-rotted animal manure. Dig it in during your September, October, digging at the rate of one barrow-load to 10 square metres (12 square yards). Compost, decomposed kitchen or garden waste, is almost as good and can be used in the same way.

Growing
From seed
It would be possible to create a virtually instant herb garden by simply going to your garden centre and buying plants. This would not only be very costly, however, but it would be very limiting. Most garden centres will stock only a small number of herb plants and since they can be grown easily from seed, in most cases, you can save yourself a great deal of money and grow a large range of plants.

Most herbs can be grown from seed, usually in spring or autumn when the weather is warm and there is no danger of frosts. Our individual listings give details of the correct method for growing each herb. Usually this involves scattering or sowing seeds in drills, covering lightly with soil and, very importantly, marking precisely where you have sown them.

Do not buy mixed herb seed since identifying them at the seedling stage will be a problem. Buy individual packets from a reputable firm and make sure that careful growing instructions are marked on the packet.

Herb plants
While it is possible to grow most herbs from seed, perennials like tarragon, rosemary, lavender and bay, will take a long time and in these cases you may prefer to buy plants. Container-grown plants can be planted at most times of the year as long as it is not too cold and there is no frost or snow. Soak the plant thoroughly, dig a hole deep enough to accomodate it and remove it from its pot or package. Place it in the hole making sure that you don't damage the roots and plant it at a level which leaves the top of its soil just below the surface of the ground. Fill with loose earth and press down firmly all round.

Propagating
Perennial plants may also be grown, renewed or increased by propagation. There are a number of techniques for this but all of them, once mastered, will save you a good deal of money in the future.

The first method is *layering*. This is the easiest method and is used for plants with flexible branches like rosemary, mint and balm. Take a strong branch close to the ground and make a slanting cut in the underside about 30cm (12 ins) from the tip. Put some hormone rooting powder on the cut and then bend the stem, still connected to the plant, so that it can be buried firmly in the soil with only the top leaves showing above the ground. Peg the stem down and leave for several weeks until roots have formed. You can then cut the stem from the main plant and place your new herb in its growing position.

The next method of propagation is *root division*. Only do this when the danger of frost is gone and the plant is dormant - autumn and early spring are best. Lift the plant and carefully separate the clump into smaller pieces. Once divided you simply replant and water well until they establish themselves. This method is, of course, only suitable for clump-forming herbs like mint.

Hard or soft wooded plants can be propagated by taking *cuttings*. Soft wood stem cuttings can be taken at any time during the growing season. Select strong stems, which show plenty of leaf, about 10 cm (4 ins) long and take off all the lower leaves. Dip each cutting (you will need several since not all will take) in water and then rooting powder. Shake off the excess powder and place in sharp sand or cutting compost. Keep the sand or compost moist, and out of direct sunlight, and the cuttings will root, according to type, in anything from four weeks to considerably longer. Be patient.

For hard wood cuttings select woody shoots of new growth and remove from the plant preferably with a "heel" of old wood from the parent plant. These are simply rooted in a sheltered spot.

Herbs in containers

If the herb is suitable for growing in a pot it can usually be grown indoors. It is best to try and maintain an even temperature and place them in a sunny spot on a window sill but not in the full glare of the sun. Feed and water during the growing season and keep the atmosphere moist. Re-pot in fresh soil each year.

All sorts of containers are suitable for growing herbs in - window boxes, hanging baskets, tubs, old sinks etc. Whatever you use, however, observe a few simple rules. Always have drainage holes, don't overcrowd them and bear in mind the eventual weight of soil and plant when you earth up the container. It might appear light when the earth is dry but when wet the weight might be too much. To ensure good drainage always cover the base with a layer of broken clay or pebbles. A good potting compost can be made up from peat, sharp sand and garden compost or loam in these proportions - 7 parts loam, 3 parts peat and one part sand. Mix together well and before planting allow the soil to settle for at least five days. When planting ensure that your pot contains plants that all enjoy the same conditions, amounts of sun and watering otherwise one, or all of them, will suffer. Most herbs can be planted in the spring but shrubby herbs like lavender, bay and rosemary can be planted at any time when they are dormant. Perennials which die-down in the winter, like the mints, will do well if they are planted in early autumn so they can get established before winter comes. If you are sowing seed, most annuals can be sown directly in spring and biennials like parsley and chervil in autumn or spring.

Watering container-grown plants is very important, even more so than those in open ground since the moisture evaporates and they can become bone dry without you realising it. Check them regularly and, if growing indoors, stand in a pot or tray of gravel to give drainage and encourage a humid atmosphere. Make sure they have plenty of light, keep them out of a draught, water regularly preferably from above, and if your central heating is likely to rob them of humidity keep a small pot of water near them. A regular application of liquid plant food will also greatly benefit them.

Picking

To collect the herbs in their best condition here are one or two tips. First, the right season and time of day are important. The best time of day is the morning. Many herbs, like mint, do not produce the ideal active constituents at night reducing the taste.

Pick from healthy, well-developed plants. Those affected by disease might be dangerous.

Always use scissors. Pulling or hacking away at plants will damage them.

Special functions

Generally the uses of herbs fall into three main categories - culinary, medicinal and cosmetic. But there are other, surprising advantages to herbs and this section aims to tell you about these less appreciated virtues.

A lot of people, for instance,

will reach instinctively for the weedkiller when they spot nettles in their garden. In most cases, of course, this would be quite understandable but in the right place and carefully controlled, nettles can bring *butterflies* into your garden to add that extra touch of life and colour. Try allowing a few nettles (Urtica dioica) to grow in a remote corner and see the results.

Hyssop, too, is a powerful attractor for butterflies and bees who enjoy its nectar and pollen. A number of herbs are attractive to bees. Bergamot, for instance, used to be called bee balm because of its heady scent and flowers bursting with honey. Balm actually disappears below ground when the bees go off to hibernate.

A number of fragrant herbs like lavender, southernwood, rosemary, mint, woodruff and curry plant can be used as *moth repellants* and at the same time, add a very pleasant smell to your clothes cupboard or linen drawers.

Either lay the herbs individually among your linen and clothes or make up a herb bag. To do this place your herbs on a piece of paper, crush under a rolling pin, add ground cloves and place the resulting mixture in nylon or cheesecloth bags. In some cases herbs would be worth growing in your garden for the *smell* alone. Acorus (Acorus calamus), when bruised, has a marvel-

lous tangerine-like smell. Peppermint (Mentha piperita) brings an unusual smell of menthol to your garden. Rosemary (Rosmarinus officinalis) has a warm mediterranean smell especially when rubbed. Thyme, especially lemon thyme (Thymus citriodorus) adds a deep, thick cloud of heavenly scent. Many more herbs like savory, woodruff and yarrow all have their own unique smells which will bestow a marvellous aroma on your garden. Why not try preserving some of these smells in petal sachets?

Lemon verbena, thyme, rosemary, lavender, marjoram, woodruff and bergamot combine with rose petals gathered fresh and unbruised when the dew has gone. Place these, dried, in muslin or taffeta bags.

You could also try making something called a Tussie Mussie which is a collection of all your favourite sweet-smelling herbs bound together in wool. They make a delightful smell and, in addition, by combining colours and shapes are attractive to look at.

If you have animals remember that they can release some of the smells of your herb garden by rubbing up against them. Why not place rows of the best-smelling herbs alongside a path where both the animals and humans brushing against them will release the smell. Cat-nip or cat-mint, when in season, can make your cat dopey with pleasure and you will find that it becomes a favourite spot for the family cat to lie. Cat-nip (Nepeta cataria) which should not be confused with Nepeta Mussini, is not an attractive plant. It grows tall and is untidy with hoary green leaves. Because of this, and the fact that your cat will sprawl underneath it, it should be planted somewhere out of the way.

If you are bothered by flies try planting either Rue (Ruta graveolens) or Tansy (Tanacetum vulgare). Rue is excellent in *repelling flies* and a tea made from it liberally sprinkled around also kills *fleas*. Tansy, also known as "buttons", has thick leaves and is also valued as a herb for repelling flies. In the garden its foliage will keep away a host of annoying insects and massaging a dog's coat with those leaves will help to keep away fleas.

Wormwood, in addition to its other uses, will discourage cabbage moths in your garden and a tea made from it and sprayed on the ground in the autumn will help to keep alway slugs and snails. It is also said to be useful in ridding domestic pets of fleas when rubbed into their coats.

Herbs have been used down the ages for a variety of *marital problems* and while no guarantees are offered for these uses readers may be intrigued by some of the more unusual applications for these most adaptable of plants.

It used to be said, for instance, that a girl who has lost her virtue before marriage could conceal this fact from her husband by having a long bath the night before the wedding night in hot water and comfrey.

A salad made from Tansy leaves is said to act as an aphrodisiac. The baser emotions of men are said to be encouraged by eating mint and at one time soldiers were actually forbidden to eat it because it took away the desire to fight. The subsequent discovery of bromide, however, may have saved this marvellous herb further victimisation.

To reduce the lusts in men the leaves of daisies, not the flowers, were once attached to their lower parts though, one suspects, the effect was achieved more from a sense of personal ridicule than by any chemical reaction.

Finally, drunkenness. Herbalists through the ages have come up with a number of treatments. Parsley seed was said to avoid the worst effects of drink and horseradish, boiled in water, was a foul way of sobering people up. If matters have gone beyond this and drunk seems beyond hope, a strong mustard emetic may well do the trick. None of these cures, however, are nearly as effective as the preventive treatment, so it seems right to turn to more sober facts now.

HERBS AND THEIR USES

In the Kitchen

The herb is truly the cook's friend and can be used to give life and flavour to almost any dish. Unfortunately it is still sadly misunderstood. Many people are either too frightened to employ it and whose serried rows of herb jars stand pristine and untouched, or have thrown overpowering handfuls of some rich herb into their cooking and forever afterwards spurned them because of the experience. Herbs are to be used in careful, controlled quantities. A recipe is not a scientific equation but it is a guide which should be followed until the cook gains the confidence of his, or her, own tastes and experiences. As you grow more confident with herbs you will undoubtedly decide which you like and which you don't, which you will want to use in quantity and which you prefer to use in modest amounts. In other words the addition of herbs will become instinctive rather than a slavishly observed ritual performed in conjunction with a cookery book.

When cooking it is clearly of benefit to have your herbs close at hand, so make sure that yours, fresh or dried, are within easy reach. Those neatly-labelled herb racks may be attractive but when you come to use them you may find that you need large quantities of some herbs, say basil and tarragon, but rarely use others. Don't be afraid to keep your herbs in different sized pots and jars according to their usage.

We have agreed that cooking is not a strict science, allowing personality, individual taste and instinct to intrude into a recipe. Science, in fact, can offer us very little help when it comes to explaining why we enjoy what we eat. The boffin may be able to describe colours or sounds accurately but ask him to define smell or taste and he's humbled, reduced to talking in terms of personal experience. This is the great thing about the enjoyment of eating - it is a purely personal thing. So remember, it is your taste which should decide how much and which herbs you use.

Bear in mind, however, that certain cooking methods have their own different effects on your herbs. Boiling, for instance in reducing a sauce, will drive away the more volatile flavourings. Long, slow cooking unleashes the more aromatic flavourings but if the lid is kept tight they will not disappear.

If you are just beginning to use herbs then it would perhaps be wise to start slowly. A basic supply useful for most beginners should include mint, sage, marjoram, rosemary, basil, tarragon, garlic, bay, thyme and chives. Some of these you can keep dried in jars but some - mint, chives and rosemary for instance -

are incomparably better fresh. It's a safe bet, however, that once you have realised what herbs can bring to your food, many of you will be growing and stocking far more.

Here are some hints for the use of herbs with various types of cooking.

Soups

Long periods of cooking tend to rob herbs of their essential flavour so add herbs individually to soups just before you have finished cooking. Experiment with your herbs to find out how best they suit various soups. Try basil, fresh or dried, with minestrone, parsley with bean soups, fennel with fish soups. You can even make a herb soup with chives, chervil, sorrel, tarragon, parsley stock and white wine.

Fish

Herbs have a variety of uses in fish cooking. They can be used to flavour the fish itself, to flavour the stock or court bouillon in which the fish is cooked or in sauces and mayonnaise which dress the fish. Bay, parsley and thyme are mostly used in fish stock. Baked fish can be sprinkled with a range of herbs, olive oil and butter then wrapped in foil and cooked. Strong cooking tends to diminish herbs so this method tends to best suit more robust herbs like rosemary and fennel. Dill is most commonly used with cold fish dishes either during the cooking or, say, in a dill sauce.

Poultry and Game

The often bland tasting chicken really needs a fine herbal ambassador to present it and tarragon is the finest herb to do this. Roast, bake or poach your chicken and then serve it with a thick, creamy tarragon sauce. Some game, especially duck and goose, puts people off because of the high fat content. But there are herbs that will counteract this. Hyssop, for instance, will combat the grease and a traditional sage and onion stuffing will also do the trick. Richer game like venison, pheasant and partridge may need something a little more assertive. Try marjoram, rosemary and thyme.

Meat

To many cooks, each type of meal has its own traditional accompaniment. Most tend to associate lamb with mint and so, too, do most types of meat have their own herb. This approach is a useful guide but can be limiting, so once you have tried the more traditional pairings - lamb with rosemary, beef with horseradish, pork with sage - try experimenting. Try shoulder of lamb with fennel, steak with oregano, veal with garlic and rosemary, pork chops with cumin. Remember, just because someone else has found a combination to his taste does not mean you should nor that you shouldn't try previously untried combinations.

Vegetables

These are probably the most neglected items of cooking after herbs. What better then, than to revive the fortunes of both with some exciting vegetable and herb recipes. Too often one tends to boil all the

life and flavour out of vegetables and serve the ensuing wreckage bland and unadorned. No vegetable should be boiled until soft. Steaming or par-boiling and steaming is a far better treatment. Good recipe books all boast plenty of interesting ways of cooking vegetables with herbs. Why not try green beans with marjoram and parsley, spinach with olive oil and garlic, beetroot with tarragon or anise, carrots with mint, cauliflower with chervil, onions in sage sauce....the list is endless.

Salads

Some cooks believe that herbs really come into their own fresh and lightly dressed without venturing anywhere near a cooker. Recipe books list salads made only with herbs like the famous nine herb salad which includes tarragon, basil, purslane, roquette, parsley, fennel and chives. Almost all herbs abundant in summer go splendidly in salads. Try cucumber salad with mint, green salad with rosemary, tarragon, thyme, anise or fennel, tomato salad with mozzarella cheese and basil or potato salad with mint and parsley.

Drying and freezing

There is little comparison between the fresh and the dried herb but there are occasions when one has to settle for the latter and especially if you have an abundance of herbs in your garden it is wise to dry your own supply. This is both cheaper and more satisfying and for the expenditure of a little time and effort you can ensure that they remain as flavoursome as possible.

The correct time to pick leaves for drying is when the flower buds begin to appear on the plant. This is the time when there is the greatest concentration of oils in the leaves and thus the strongest flavour. Pick small-leaved herbs like tarragon, rosemary and thyme by the branch and hang them up to dry in bundles, Those with larger leaves can be picked individually. In each case pick only the best, un-bruised, leaves in the morning when the dew has gone.

Those tied in bundles should be hung to dry in a warm dry place like an airing cupboard and put in bottles or jars when they become brittle. Larger-leafed herbs can be placed on a tray, covered with kitchen paper and dried in similar conditions. Turn them periodically to ensure even drying. When brittle crush and store in jars.

Herbs are ideal for freezing and this often preserves the taste far more effectively. Delicate varieties like basil and dill can be picked by the stems and wrapped in cling film before freezing. Parsley can be chopped and placed in plastic

bags. Other herbs can be chopped, mixed with water and poured into ice trays.

Teas and other drinks

Herbs provide the basis for many drinks, both hot and cold, which are refreshing and which sometimes have a history shrouded in magic and witchcraft.

Many can be given to children, invalids and the elderly as a general health-giving drink which provides them with a good source of valuable vitamins in an easily-digested form. One of the commonest is mint tea. Either peppermint or spearmint can be used and the quantity of leaves will decide the strength. Take about 8 tablespoons of mint, either chopped or roughly torn, place in a teapot (though perhaps not the one you regularly use for normal tea) and pour on a pint of boiling water. Leave for the mixture to infuse and serve after 5 minutes. Sweeten with a little sugar or honey. Herbal drinks can give a great deal of pleasure in addition to doing you good. Sipping apple juice with mint, tomato juice with basil or fruit juice with parsley makes a very refreshing change. Perhaps the commonest use of herbs in drinks, however, is in the cocktail, punch or wine cup. Strong mediterranean wines like those from Algeria, Portugal and Southern Spain often don't have the taste to be served on their own but will make the basis of a very pleasant wine cup - with the additional advantage that they go further in this fashion.

Try a wine cup with two bottles of wine, half a bottle of sherry, two slices of cucumber, a pint of soda water, two tablespoons of cointreau (optional), apple slices and sprigs of borage. Mix the wine, sherry, liquer and cucumber together and chill. Just before serving add soda water, pour into a large jug and adorn with cucumber, apple and borage.

In England borage is probably best known for its appearance in that ubiquitous summer drink Pimms. Too many people, when serving Pimms, go overboard with the vegetation leaving the drink resembling one of the more impenetrable areas of an Amazonian rain forest.

Borage and mint, or for that matter any of the herbal additions, can really spoil a summer drink when used in too great a quantity.

The lessons of cooking with herbs apply equally to making drinks.

Easy does it!

Talking of alcohol brings us onto the drinks you can brew yourself with the addition of herbs. Elder (Sambucus nigra) produces flowers and berries which make a heady wine. If using the berries remember that they are strong on tannin which will make them quite harsh unless allowed to mature for a couple of years.

Preserving

For centuries herbs have been used in preserving vegetables, meats and other foods. They add a depth and flavour which, combined with a preserving agent like vinegar, keeps your produce edible and flavoursome.

Remember, however, that there is no point in trying to keep something that is on its last legs. Poor produce preserved will always be poor produce no matter what you do to it. Try and always select the best whether you are pickling gherkins, making a chutney or simply marinading a leg of lamb that you want to keep for a week. Preserving is the art of retaining all the best qualities of your produce so that an onion will remain crisp and tangy, a beetroot firm and slightly woody. Whatever you choose to preserve your food in will add an extra taste to it but it should not mask the basic taste of that which you are preserving.

For this reason always try and use wine vinegar, unless you are making a powerful chutney or relish, instead of malt vinegar. The taste of malt vinegar is robust and overwhelming and may spoil the flavour of more delicate produce.

In most cases preserving requires a marriage between vinegar and herbs - a most fortunate thing since wine vinegar has a remarkable ability to draw out the best in herbs.

Vinegars

Herb vinegars are beginning to appear in the shops, tarragon vinegar being the most common, but with very little trouble you can make your own which will always be made from the freshest herbs and have the advantage of being considerably cheaper. To make tarragon vinegar all you need is a pint of tarragon leaves, a pint of white wine vinegar heated, two cloves and one garlic clove sliced in half. Rub the tarragon leaves lightly in the hands so as to crumble them, add the vinegar, cloves and garlic and cover the mixture and allow it to stand for a day. Take out the garlic and let the mixture stand for another two weeks. After this time strain and press through a cloth. Bottle and cork. To make it that little bit more special try adding a long slender tarragon leaf to the bottle. A herb oil is equally simple to make. For basil oil - excellent with pizzas or in making pasta sauces - all you need is four tablespoons of the herb, lightly chopped, and three quarters of a pint of olive oil. In a mortar pound the basil, add a little of the oil and continue to pound. Steadily mix in all the oil and then pour into a wide mouthed bottle. Seal and leave for a couple of weeks before using.

Pickling

One of the best reasons for preserving, however, is so that we can enjoy those marvellous

tangy pickles and chutneys that make a salad, a slice of cold meat, a pie or even a thick slab of cheese so delicious. Good herbs for pickling include fennel, coriander, mint and dill.

A great deal of hokum is talked about pickling. Recipes allegedly passed from generation to generation are guarded with a secrecy quite beyond their merit.

You would think that preserving the humble onion and beetroot was almost a magical art rather than a straightforward affair.

Pickling is quite simply preserving something in vinegar and is done in two simple stages. First, you prepare very carefully that which you are going to pickle ensuring that you have chosen only the best. The second step is to create the pickling agent which covers that which you are pickling. A magnificent and slightly unusual example is this recipe for garlic dill gherkins.

Wash small, tender gherkins and fill your jars (however many you need) with them. Mix a quart of white wine or cider vinegar with three quarts of water and one cup of salt. Bring to the boil. Into each jar scatter several heads of dill and several cloves of garlic sliced in half. Fill the jars with the boiling vinegar and water mixture and seal while still reasonably hot. Leave for about three weeks and then devour.

Chutneys

Chutneys are equally simple to make involving a marriage between vinegar, sugar, herbs, spices and your chosen vegetables. Chutneys need long, slow cooking so need more robust herbs. You would also be wise to make the chutney mixture which will be eaten much later a little runnier than that which you will eat first. Chutney tends to dry up and if you make a large quantity the final few jars could be very dry otherwise.

Try apple and mint chutney. Mix together one pound of crisp apples (chopped), half a pound of seedless raisins, two small onions (chopped), half a pound of chopped tomatoes, two large red peppers (chopped), one pound of sugar, two tablespoons of salt, two tablespoons of dry mustard and a good handful of chopped spearmint and coriander leaves. Place all this in an earthenware pot and pour over them two quarts of wine vinegar which has been boiled and left to cool. Leave for several days, stirring occasionally, and then bottle. It will keep without sealing but this will tend to make it dry up quicker.

For the smell

We already know of the delights that herbs can give, with their heady smell, in the garden. But, gathered and prepared properly you can have sweet-scented collections of herbs all over the house.

Pot pourris, pomander balls, cushions, lavender – bags there is a wide variety of different techniques for capturing the essential aroma of herbs and of releasing them in your home.

Pot pourris

A pot pourri, perhaps the most familiar device on that list, is a mixture of dried, sweet-smelling herbs, spices and petals, occasionally also containing oils and spirits, all combined in such a fashion that you have a long-lasting delicate aroma wafting about your home.

Once you have established a few ground rules about the making of pot pourris then you can largely follow your own instincts. Always make sure that petals and leaves are properly dried, this will preserve their smell and colour. A

pot pourri must look attractive as well as smell delightful, therefore select some brightly-coloured buds and flowers from your garden and, even if they do not smell strongly, dry these too.

A pot pourri can either be dry or moist.

The latter, usually made with orange peel, is best stored in those perforated china jars.

Made up carefully and stored in this way they can last for years and years.

Dry pot pourris are simply kept in open bowls of any kind. To make a pot pourri you must gather strong scented rose petals when dry and spread out individually on paper in an airy room.

Gather your other flowers and herbs - lemon verbena, peppermint, lemon balm, rosemary, lavender, violets, chamomile and a host of other sweet-smelling plants are ideal - dry them and mix in a bowl. Add a fixative, usually common salt in moist pot pourris and orris root or gum benzoin in dry ones, to stop evaporation of the essential oils and to preserve the smell and blend the fragrances. Then add a selection of spices either crushed or ground. Choose from powerful, heady ones like coriander, nutmeg, cloves or vanilla pod.

Pomander balls

Pomander balls, sometimes called clove oranges, can be splendid Christmas presents and can be hung up in a cupboard or placed in drawers. They will deter moths and give your clothes and linen a pleasant smell.

To make a pomander ball take one of the thin-skinned oranges, stick it full of cloves and roll it in a mixture of one teaspoon of orris powder and one of ground cinnamon. Wrap the orange in tissue paper and leave for two weeks in a dark cupboard. Remove the orange, shake well to remove any surplus and tie a ribbon round it if you are going to hang it up.

Herb cushions

Herb pillows or cushions can be made with dried sweet-smelling herbs and have traditionally been used to soothe the nerves and induce sleep. Take a piece of cheesecloth and cut it up to form the shape of a small pillow. Sew up three sides and select dried crushed herbs - sage, peppermint, lavender, marjoram, woodruff, rosemary and other sweet herbs are ideal - with which you fill the pillow. Add a couple of drops of essential oil, maybe rose or lavender or even a couple of drops of vodka, so the herbs do not rustle inside and disturb your sleep. Sew up the fourth side and there's your herb pillow.

If you suffer from headaches you can make up a special pillow with equal quantities of soothing herbs like peppermint, spearmint and bergamot, fixing them with orris root.

Lavender bags

Lavender is probably the most familiar herbal smell and has been used for generations to give rooms, clothes and linen a pleasant smell while at the same time driving away moths. But it's not just lavender that will do this. Southernwood, rosemary, mint, woodruff and curry plant among others also discourage moths. They can all be used in moth bags.

To make a moth bag simply cut up cotton cloth into small bags some three inches square and use the dried herbs on their own or mixed with a crushed spice like cinnamon to increase their power and life. Alternatively make triangular coat hanger-shaped bags and fill them in the same fashion.

Dyeing

In ancient times man used herbs not just to cook and cure but also in rough dyeing. In the same way that the process of trial and error helped him to discover what was safe to eat and what was a useful treatment for his ailments he also discovered that some herbs had the ability to give new colour to his clothes. Many other plants have this ability but there are quite sufficient herbs to achieve a satisfying result in most colours.

Just spare a thought for early man, however, in his experiments.

How did he discover the right herbs and more particularly how did he discover that some other materials held the dye fast? It must have been a laborious process.

This colour-fast property of some materials – *mordants* – is crucial to most effective dyeing. The word 'mordant' comes from the Latin verb meaning 'to bite'. Natural dyes are either substantive, which means they need no mordant or they are adjective in which case they do. This section contains a comprehensive list of herbs, their respective mor-

HERB	PART USED	MORDANT	COLOUR
ANGELICA	Whole plant	Copper	Mid-green
		Iron	Darker green
CHAMOMILE	Flowers	Alum and CT *	Bright yellow
CENTAURY	Tops	Alum and CT	Yellow
CHICORY	Leaves	Copper and soda	Burnt orange
DANDELION	Flowers	Alum	Bright yellow
		Tin or chrome	Orange
ELECAMPANE	Root	Wood ash	Blue
ELDER	Leaves and twigs	Copper and Iron	Green
	Fruit	Vinegar	Blue/purple
FENNEL	Tops	Copper	Bronze
		Iron	Brown
FENUGREEK	Seeds	Alum and CT	Yellow
HOP	Tops and stalks	No mordant	Browns and reds
HORSERADISH	Tops	Alum	Yellow
	Leaves	Chrome	Deep yellow
IRIS	Roots	Iron	Black
	Flowers	Alum	Yellow
JUNIPER	Berries	Alum and CT	Olive brown
	Tops	Alum and CT	Mauve brown
LILY OF THE VALLEY	Leaves	Chrome	Olive green
		Copper	Green
MARJORAM	Tops	Alum	Green
		Chrome	Olive green
MULLEIN	Tops	Copper	Green
		Iron	Dark green
ST JOHN'S WORT	Stalks	Alum	Yellow
	Flowers	Alum	Yellow
SAFFRON	Stigma	Alum and CT	Yellow
		Tin	Bright yellow
SAGE	Tops	Alum and CT	Yellow
		Copper	Green
SORREL	Tops	Amonia	Dark olive
		Vinegar	Pinks
TANSY	Tops	Alum and CT	Yellow
YARROW	Whole plant	Copper	Bronze

* CT = cream of tartar

dants and the colours their natural dyes will give to your clothes.

Dyes can be made from the flowers, leaves, stalks and roots of herbs and here is a rough guide to the respective quantities and methods.

Flowers: allow twice the weight of flowers to that of fibre or material. Pick when in full bloom. Soak in water for an hour then simmer for another hour. Strain off the flowers and use the liquid as the dye bath.

Leaves and Stalks: allow twice the weight of leaves and stalks to that of fibre or material. Soak in water for up to three days to break them down and then simmer for an hour. Strain and use the liquid as a dye bath.

Roots: allow at least twice the weight of roots to that of fibre or material. Soak for up to seven days to break them down and then simmer gently. Strain and use the liquid as the dye bath.

Physical care

Walk into any chemist or beauty aid shop and you will find herbs leaping at you from the labels on almost every bottle and jar. The multi-billion pound cosmetics industry has recognised the commercial advantages of associating the products with herbs. It gives them a "natural" image.

When you buy a jar, bottle or tube, whether it's for hair shampoo or a face cream, remember that you are paying a sizeable sum for the glossy packaging and the costly advertising campaigns. It's perfectly easy to make cheap, effective beauty preparations at home using fresh or dried herbs and other common kitchen ingredients. Home-made cosmetic treatments are not only cheaper and give you tremendous satisfaction but they also give you the peace of mind that comes from knowing what is in them. Preservatives in modern cosmetic aids often contain chemicals which create reactions with the skin. Home-made preparations do not contain these preservatives though this also means that they will not last as long as shopbought ones.

Home-made treatments can be used to care for almost every part of your body so lets's start at the top and work downwards.

Hair

The appearance of your hair is a surprisingly good indicator of your general health. A good hairdresser will often know as much about your health from the condition of your hair as your doctor might from a cursory examination. Herbal shampoos won't make your hair healthy, a good diet is probably the best way of ensuring that, but they will give you a safe, effective and enjoyable way of washing your hair. For a basic herbal shampoo make an infusion of soapwort leaves (Saponaria officinalis), simmer gently for five minutes, strain and use in conjunction with an infusion of any other of a variety of herbs like rosemary, nettle, chamomile or southernwood in the proportions of three parts soapwort infusion to one part of other herb. The latter infusion must be strong. Make with half a cup of water and at least two tablespoons of herb. Let it cool before mixing with the soapwort.

After shampooing use a herbal rinse made with sage or rosemary for dark hair and chamomile or yarrow for light hair.

Dandruff is most commonly nothing more than dry flaking of the scalp and indicates a lack of regular brushing. If you do suffer from dandruff, however, make up a shampoo with two egg whites, one tablespoon of soft soap and one tablespoon of strong infusion of nettle leaves made by pouring half a cup of boiling water onto one heaped tablespoon of nettles.

Face

There are so many aspects to the herbal treatment of the face that one could write a complete book on the subject. However, here is a simple, basic skin cleansing lotion as an indication of the way herbs can help to care for your face. For dry and normal skin take one ounce of lanolin and cocoa butter, add four tablespoons of sweet almond oil and place in a bowl over boiling water to melt. Cool slightly and add four tablespoons of a strong infusion of herbs. Those which are good for dry skin are borage, comfrey, fennel and marigold. Blend all the ingredients and store in a screwtop jar. Shake well before use. For those with oily skin take half a pint of milk and add it to three tablespoons of chopped herbs. Those that are good for oily skin are nettle, rosemary, sage, yarrow and chamomile. Warm until you can smell the herb strongly but don't allow it to boil. Cool and strain into a screwtop jar.

Eyes

To soothe tired eyes and to make them brighter there are a number of herbal treatments. Herbs that are good for eyes include eyebright (Euphrasia officinalis) which, as its name suggests, is good for almost all eye troubles. Also elderflower, fennel and wormwood can be used. For a basic eye compress soak lint pads in a cold infusion of any of these herbs, squeeze lightly and place over the eyes. Rest for ten minutes refreshing the lint when it gets warm.

Hands

The biggest problem with most people's hands comes not from some medical trouble but from the ravages of cold weather and from day to day activities like washing up. As a remedy to this a good basic hand rinse can be made from any one of a number of herbs that are kind to hands like fennel, marigold, comfrey and chamomile.

Make an infusion with one pint of boiling water over two tablespoons of the herb. You can also make a cream using the herbs. For example, fennel cream is made with a strong infusion made from one table-spoon of the herb and half a cup of boiling water.

Cool and strain. Blend two teaspoons of arrowroot, two tablespoons of glycerine, two tablespoons of lavender water and the fennel infusion. Stir over a gentle heat until thick and store in a screwtop jar.

Feet

Tired feet are one of the com-monest problems, and no wonder considering what we put our feet through in a day and the kind of shoes that many of us make our feet work in. Never fear, there are herbs that are kind to the feet like mugwort, burdock, marigold and comfrey. Add as much as possible of your chosen herb to half a pint of sweet almond oil and leave for three weeks in a warm place shaking regularly. Heat the oil mixture in a pan until herbs become brittle and then cool, strain and bottle. Massage your tired feet with the mixture whenever neces-sary.

Baths. There is nothing like a good, relaxing bath and once again herbs can come to your aid. A herbal bath can be simply a relaxing experience but herbs are also capable of toning up the skin and stimu-lating and correcting skin disorders.

The best way to add herbs to your bath without a messy, inconvenient collection of herbs washing around you is to make herb bags from pieces of cheesecloth with a draw-string. Hang these on the hot tap so that the water flows through them. The other method would be to make a strong infusion and simply add to the bath.

For a simple herbal bath tonic try comfrey or nettle. Other excellent bath herbs are thyme, marigold, lavender, chamomile, lovage or rose-mary.

Health

Though suspicion still lingers among the more conservative in the medical world an in-creasing number of doctors now accept that there are many cases where herbal re-medies provide a safe, natural and often more succesful opti-on.

Ever since herbs were first used a process of trial and error has shown their benefits in treating disease and physi-cal ailments.

Among the earliest texts known to man, the Ebers Pa-pyrus from 1550 BC, shows how the ancient Egyptians used herbs in medicine and reveals that they had a re-markably good understanding of how both they and the hu-man body worked.

From then, through the ancient Greeks, Hippocrates in the 5th century BC, the classical herbalist Dioscorides in the 1st century AD, the monks of the Middle Ages, right up until the present day, herbs have been used for health. To ignore this fact, or to treat this body of knowledge as the unsophisticated meddling of untutored minds, is to shut out a valuable collected wisdom which even the most brilliant scientists are unable to ignore. When pharmacology was merely an infant science the discoveries of the herbalists were laying down a basis upon which modern medicine was to proceed. Medical science, in all its modern, sophisticated glory, was born out of the desire to study, observe and learn from the effects of plant chemicals upon the body. The first, faltering steps of modern medicine grew out of experiments to distil the essential oils from herbs to use as remedies. So, while medical science has progressed by leaps and bounds since those days many of its discoveries originate in applications which may be no less effective now than they were all those years ago.

Herbal remedies are easy to understand, use and even

make, given a local supply of the herbs, and if used in the correct dosages can prove remarkably efficient.

Take care

It is, however, vital when using herbal remedies to follow the instructions carefully. The power of herbs lies in the fact that they contain chemicals and taking them in large or prolonged doses can have the same poisonous effect as an overdose of modern chemicals.

Some herbs also have **side effects** and here is a list of the more common and when they should be avoided.

Elder - poisonous berries, should not be eaten raw.

Hop - should not be taken for more than 2-3 weeks.

Juniper - not to be taken during pregnancy.

Horseradish - not to be taken for more than 2-3 weeks, during pregnancy or by people with kidney problems.

Hyssop - not to be taken for more than 2-3 weeks.

Lovage - not to be taken during pregnancy or by those with kidney problems.

Pot Marjoram - not during pregnancy or with kidney problems.

Rosemary - not to be taken for more than 2-3 weeks.

Yarrow - extended use may make skin sensitive to light.

Sage - not to be taken for more than 2-3 weeks.

Wormwood - excessive use increases blood circulation in the mucus membrane of the stomach and causes vertigo. Not to be taken during pregnancy.

Liquorice - taken for too long can lead to water retention.

Watercress - excessive amounts irritate the urinary passage.

Parsley - not to be taken by those with kidney problems or during pregnancy.

Rue - harmful in large doses. Increases the blood flow to smooth muscle so not to be taken during pregnancy.

In explaining the medicinal application of herbs a number of **terms** are used regularly and here is an explanation of the commonest.

Infusion

A tea made by pouring boiling water over the herbs and then allowing the mixture to steep for ten minutes. Strain and serve. When described as a tea it should be drunk hot, when as an infusion it should be drunk luke warm or cold.

Compress

A clean piece of cloth or towelling soaked in the infusion or decoction, wrung out and applied to the affected area.

Decoction

A method used to extract ingredients from the harder parts of a herb. These are usually crushed, scraped, chopped or grated before boiling up in water for ten minutes and then steeped for another ten minutes. Leave to cool before straining off liquid.

Poultice

Made with crushed or chopped herbs, heated and

applied directly to the affected part. Place in a piece of muslin or cloth, immerse in boiling water until the herb is soft, wring out and apply. Can be heated up two or three times before it loses its goodness.

Ointment
Mix two ounces (50g) of crushed herb with eight ounces (200g) of either pure lard or white petroleum jelly and simmer for 20 minutes. Strain into a screwtop jar.

Tincture
This uses alcohol instead of water so that it will keep indefinitely. Take one and a half ounces (40g) of powdered herb to one pint (580ml) of rubbing alcohol or vodka. Place in an airtight jar in a warm place, shaking periodically, for three or four weeks. Strain and store.

Ever since man started to observe the effects of herbs he has built up a body of knowledge about their behaviour. But it wasn't until fairly recently that scientists were able to endorse many of the claimed applications of herbs. One of the most remarkable is feverfew (Tanacetum parthenium). For centuries it has been hailed as a cure for headache and rheumatism. More recently migraine sufferers started to chew the leaf of the herb and officials at the London Migraine Clinic began to record some impressive results. A long-term study of 250 takers was launched and it showed that on taking a leaf a day for three months some 70 per cent of the takers recorded a significant reduction in the frequency or severity of attacks.

Ailments
Here are some other common ailments and the herbal treatments used to deal with them.

Acne. Warm infusions of coltsfoot, elder, hop, marshmallow, thyme, sorrel or valerian applied as a compress.

Colds. Hot infusions of borage chamomile, elder or horseradish. Inhaling balsam or chamomile will relieve stuffiness.

Constipation. Warm infusions of dandelion, feverfew, basil, chickweed or fennel.

Coughs. A tea made from mullein flowers or a syrup made from the stems of Angelica.

Ear-ache. A few drops of a warm infusion of chamomile flowers or fennel leaves.

Eyes. An infusion of eyebright applied as a cold compress eases tired and sore eyes.

Headache. Various herb teas suit the various types of headache and trial and error is perhaps the best method of deciding which best suits you. Remember the use of feverfew referred to earlier. Any herb from: eyebright, rose, sage, savory, thyme, woodruff and yarrow.

Insomnia. Sleep inducing herbs taken in a hot tea just before sleep include elderflower, bergamot, chamomile and hop.

Stomach ache. An infusion of peppermint or fenugreek.

ABOUT THE LISTED HERBS

Over the next fifty-three pages you will be able to find a comprehensive guide to one hundred and six different herbs. Some are culinary, some are medical, some cosmetic and some largely ornamental. There may even be some which you would not strictly regard as herbs but are included for their flavouring uses. We have selected such a large range of herbs in order to illustrate just how varied are the uses of herbs, and while our list is not exhaustive it should cover all the herbs you are likely to come across or need to use.

This section provides a full-colour photograph of each herb so that it can be properly identified and so that you will know, when planting, how it will look in your herb garden. There is also a potted biography of the herb giving some of the history, where it comes from and a general description. Each listing also contains details of the flowering period, the colour and the height to which it grows. All this is important should you be planning a herb garden. It will enable you to plan properly what should go where. You would not want to plant a tall, heavily-flowering herb in front of a small delicate one. Nor would you want to plant a herb which gives you a glorious early splash of colour behind one which has a bushy, evergreen foliage. Carefully study these details. But also,

when planting, you will need to know details of how to grow your herbs. Most seed packets from reputable firms will give details but our listings include advice on growing, what soil they like, whether they like sun or shade and how to propagate them. Advice on general techniques in propagation can be found in the chapter 'Herbs in the garden.' Some herbs will be delicate and will require great care though most need only a good start and they will grow happily despite the fact that many hail from more exotic – and warm – parts. Some will need, for this reason, to be brought inside over the winter, others will need careful watching if they are not to grow rampant in your garden. All these details and more you can find in these listings.

In addition to this we tell you about their uses, whether culinary, cosmetic, medicinal, in dyeing or as ornamental plants. These uses will refer, in many cases, to other sections of the book. For instance, where we say a herb should be used in an infusion the explanation of an infusion can be found in the section on health. In other cases we will talk about uses in cooking and reference may be made to the section on culinary uses of herbs. What follows is probably one of the most comprehensive guides to herbs available in the shops. We hope you find it useful and enjoyable.

ACHILLEA millefolium
Yarrow

Flowering period: early summer to autumn.
Colour: white or pink(flowers), dark green(leaves).
Height: up to 60 cm.
A native of Europe this hardy perennial is commonly found in open grassland. A versatile plant it is said to have been used by Achilles to heal wounds. Folklore has it that if a girl's nose bleeds when tickled with yarrow her love is true.
Care: Plant in spring or autumn from a rooted plant found in the wild. Easy to grow it requires little care once found a spot in open sun or partial shade. It can be grown from root division.
Uses: Young leaves in small quantities can be added to salads and it can be used instead of hops in brewing. Yarrow tea helps lack of appetite and indigestion. An infusion of the flowers makes a lotion for greasy skin. Chewing fresh leaves soothes toothache.

ACORUS calamus
Sweet Flag

Flowering period: June to July.
Colour: greenish-brown(flowers).
Height: 1-1½ metres.
A perennial not native to northern Europe and brought here from the Arab countries after the crusades. It is found commonly at the water's edge around lakes and marshes. Stout rhizome-like roots and great sword-like leaves give off a tangerine smell when bruised. It was used when quinine ran out during the Crimean War to ward off marsh pestilence.
Care: Propagate by simple division of clumps of rhizomes in early autumn and, surprisingly for a plant found in boggy areas, it will get on in comparatively dry soil.
Uses: Dried root-stalks make an infusion which is used as an emetic. The rubbed herb can be used as a soothing device for wounds. It contains an aromatic, etheric oil and has a bitter taste. That is why it works as an ermetic – it affects the intestines in such a way as to rinse them thoroughly. In the garden Sweet Flag is used to beautify ditches and other wet places where many plants don't prosper.

ALLIUM sativum
Garlic

Flowering period: June to August.
Colour: white(flowers), green(leaves).
Height: up to 60 cm.
Garlic's health-giving powers have
been exploited since pyramid workers
were kept fit on it. A perennial bulb
which consists of underground
bulblets known as cloves, it is encased
in a tough, papery-white, skin.
Care: Plant in individual cloves in late
February or March, again in November
if desired, 5 cm deep and 15 cm apart
in moist soil and a sunny spot.
It grows best in a light soil, enriched
with some well-rotted, moisture-
retentive material
Water well if dry and harvest in August
or September when leaves die down.
Uses: Used sparingly it imparts a
magnificent flavour to all savoury
dishes especially lamb and salads.
Eating garlic wards off colds and aids
the intestines, kidneys and chest
through its antiseptic qualities. It also
lowers blood pressure.

ALLIUM schoenoprasum
Chives

Flowering period: June and July.
Colour: silvery pink(flowers), green-
(leaves).
Height: 30-40 cm.
A hardy perennial member of the onion
family which is among the easiest of all
plants to grow. Attractive flowers and
thin, tubular-like leaves.
Care: Can be grown from seed but it is
far easier to buy plants. Place in a herb
bed 20 cm apart in rich, damp soil and
a sunny spot. Allow to multiply but
every three to four years divide clumps
and re-plant. Removing flower-heads
keeps flavour in the leaves. Can be
winter-grown indoors in pots.
Uses: Chopped in salads, sprinkled on
potatoes, egg dishes, cheese and on
hot dishes at the last moment. Mildly
laxative it aids digestion. Never bring
chives to the boil since this will not
only diminish the flavour but also the
laxative effects.

ALTHAEA officinalis
Marshmallow

Flowering period: late summer to
early autumn.
Colour: pale pink and white(flowers).
Height: up to 1.2 metres.
Used as a vegetable in Roman times
this hardy perennial was still boiled
and eaten in Europe until fairly recently. Now it is mainly grown for medicinal reasons.
Care: Sow ripe seeds in autumn in
deeply-dug, enriched, soil in a moist
spot. Thin to 45 cm apart and protect
with a top dressing in winter. May also
be propagated by root division in
spring or autumn.
Uses: An infusion of leaves makes a
gargle for soothing throats and also a
drink for bronchial and gastric problems. Boiled, grated, roots can be
used in an eyewash and for digestive
and urinary problems. The root is also
used in a face pack for dry skin. Use
chopped leaves sparingly in salads.

ANETHUM graveolens
Dill

Flowering period: July to September.
Colour: deep yellow(flowers), bluish-
green(leaves).
Height: up to 90 cm.
An annual from southern Europe, it
was popular with Ancient Greeks and
Romans. The name comes from the
Norse (dilla) meaning to lull, illustrat-
ing its reputation as a soothing herb.
In the Middle Ages it was also used to
drive away witches.
Care: Sow in April to June progres-
sively, to ensure a succession of
young leaves, in good, well-drained
soil and in a sunny spot. Seeds are
sown in drills and thinned to 30 cm
apart. Leaves are ready for picking in
eight weeks after sowing.
Uses: Use dill leaves fresh in salads,
sauces and with chicken, veal, soups
and in mayonnaise. Use dried brown
seeds in pickling. Dill seed tea makes a
soothing drink and used as a hand
rinse it strengthens nails. It can also
be used as a gripe water to stop hic-
coughs and induce sleep in babies. An
infusion of seeds acts as a tranquillizer
and relieves upset stomachs. Chew
the seeds to sweeten the breath.

ANGELICA archangelica
Angelica

Flowering period: June to August.
Colour: greenish-white(flowers).
Height: up to 2 metres.
Sadly this useful perennial or biennial is not grown very much any more. It can sometimes be found in damp meadows and coastal areas and was once said to have magical powers. It is named after Archangel Michael because it was said to bloom on May 8 when he appeared in a famous vision.
Care: Sow seeds in March or April in groups where it is to flower, one metre apart, in rich partially shaded soil. Thin out to retain the strongest. Sometimes the flowers do not appear until the third or fourth year. Note the height to which it grows and place in an accordingly suitable spot.
Uses: Young stems and leaf-stalks are used for crystallizing in cakes and sweets. Angelica tea, from leaves and stalks, reduces tension and aids colds and flatulence. Fresh leaves in a poultice help gout and rheumatism. Use leaves for flavouring fish, salads, stewed rhubarb and in marmalade. Similarities with juniper make it suitable for use in flavouring gin.

ANTHEMIS nobilis
Common chamomile

Flowering period: June to August.
Colour: white(flowers).
Height: up to 15-22 cm.
A perennial plant of the chamomile family commonly grown in Europe for small, fragant lawns and other ground cover uses. This dwarf species needs little cutting though, if used for ground cover, it should not be allowed to flower.
Care: Propagate by division and cuttings in April. Plants should be placed 10 cm apart. It can also be sown in boxes and planted out when 5 cm high. Sow in staggered rows at 80 plants to the square metre if grown for ground cover. Hand weed.
Uses: If allowed to flower an infusion of dried flowers makes a mouthwash and a soothing tea for stomach upsets. Used in a wash or compress it helps skin rashes.

ANTHRISCUS cerefolium
Chervil

Flowering period: May to July.
Colour: white(flowers), light-green(leaves).
Height: up to 50 cm.
A hardy perennial famous in France and other parts of Europe for flavouring, this herb was brought to England by the Romans who admired its blood-cleansing and diuretic qualities.
Care: In order to enjoy this herb all the year round sow steadily from March to late summer a few seeds at a time. It is not fussy about soil type but likes well-drained spots in partial shade. It can be container-grown. Thin seedlings to 15 cm apart and pick 6 to 8 weeks later. Bolting, fading in sunlight or letting it get too dry will rob it of flavour.
Uses: Chervil provides one of the basic flavours in the classic 'fines herbes' mixture from French cooking. Its soft, anise-tasting, leaves go well in sauces, scrambled eggs, soups and salads. An infusion of leaves is useful as a cleansing lotion for skin and in relieving flatulence and catarrh. Apply juice from leaves to stings and bites.

APIUM graveolens
Celery

Flowering period: insignificant.
Colour: pale-green(leaves).
Height: 30-45 cm.
A hardy perennial vegetable-come-herb which some may be surprised to find in this book. However, it was very popular as a herb with the Romans.
Care: Grow in an open, sunny position in well drained soil. Prepare well-manured 30 cm trenches in winter and plant in late May or June in the trenches. Keep well-watered and remove any side growths from the base. Earth-up trenches when plants are 30-45 cm high. Tie stems loosely below the leaves and fill up round each plant to form a slope of soil half way up the stem. Continue to earth up at two to three-week intervals, and in December place straw over late-maturing plants to protect against frost.
Uses: Used along with lovage as a flavouring and to make celery salt. Celery seeds are commonly used in cooking especially in soups and stews.

ARTEMISIA absinthium
Wormwood

Flowering period: July and August.
Colour: yellow(flowers), silver-
grey(leaves).
Height: up to 90 cm.
A shrubby, deciduous perennial native
to Europe and traditionally said to have
flourished along the serpent's path in
the Garden of Eden. It was highly-
prized by apothecaries and botanists
down the ages and once used as an
antidote to the poison hemlock.
Care: Sow seed in spring or autumn or
propagate by cuttings or root division
at these times. Wormwood likes light,
well-drained soil and a sunny spot.
Uses: Its unique, bitter taste is an
important ingredient in Chartreuse or
Pernod but beware, its essential oil is a
narcotic poison which used to account
for the lives of many an absinthe
drinker. Boiled, wormwood is useful
for combating worms, especially tape
worms. It can also be used in a poultice to treat ringworm. In cooking use
very sparingly to flavour roast lamb,
goose or duck and boiled pork. Prolonged use of Wormwood should be
avoided and it should not be taken at
all during pregnancy.

ARTEMISIA dracunculus
French Tarragon

Flowering period: Mid to late summer.
Colour: white or pale yellow(flowers).
Height: up to 1 metre.
The basis of so many dishes that no
herb collection should be without it. A
perennial shrub native to central Asia it
grows, under the right conditions, in
Europe. Unlike many herbs this one
stands on its culinary virtues alone.
Care: Like most aristocratic plants
Tarragon requires careful attention.
Since it won't set seed in temperate
climes this perennial shrub must be
grown from plants or by taking cuttings of rooted shoots taken in the
spring. It needs a sunny, sheltered
position and well-drained soil. Plant
30 cm apart and feed in the growing
season. Every four years divide plants.
Uses: Excellent with chicken, fish and
eggs and in light sauces and mayonnaise and soups. Fresh sprigs are
used in Tarragon vinegar. It can also
be used in an infusion to aid digestion
and in a herb pillow to help sleep.

ARTEMISIA vulgaris
Mugwort

Flowering period: July to September.
Colour: purple or dull yellow(flowers).
Height: 60-120 cm.
A hardy perennial shrub with dark green leaves, hairy on the underside, and purplish red stems. Leaves are variable in size and shape. It has oblong, reddish flower heads more slender than other artemisias like wormwood. Common in hedges and other waste places.
Care: Can be grown on almost any type of soil. Propagate by division and plant with at least 60 cm each side. Harvest flower shoots between July and September.
Uses: Makes a splendid foot bath when used as an infusion. An insect repellant it is used in moth bags combined with other sweet-smelling herbs. An aromatic culinary herb it can be used in vegetable salads. Long used to aid diarrhoea. It is said that walking with mugwort in the shoes will mean your feet never get tired. It is excellent used sparingly with either meat or salad.

ASPERULA odorata
Woodruff

Flowering period: early summer.
Colour: white(flowers) dark-green(leaves).
Height: up to 20 cm.
A perennial creeping woodland plant which has the fragrance of new-mown hay, which becomes more pronounced when cut and dried. Historically it has been used to flavour wines and placed, dried, in linen to keep away moths. Leaves are in whorls of six, dark-green and pointed. Flowers are bell or funnel-shaped and last only a short while.
Care: Sow late in summer in ordinary soil and a shady spot. Plants should be thinned to 20 cm apart. Though slow to germinate Woodruff spreads quite quickly by root runners. It can also be propagated by root division.
Uses: Excellent for ground cover under large shrubs. Woodruff tea made from dried leaves and flowers helps stomach pains, insomnia, migraine and nervous problems. Dried leaves and flowers can be used in herb pillows and pot pourris. Dried leaves added to wine cups or apple juice impart extra flavour.

ATRIPLEX hortensis
Saltbush

Flowering period: Insignificant.
Colour: purple leaves.
Height: 180 cm.
One of the many plants the leaves of
which can be used as a substitute for
spinach. It is rarely grown for that
purpose any more however.
A native of Asia it is grown more
nowadays as an ornamental plant
which reaches a height of six feet or
more and produces striking dark red
or purple arrow-shaped leaves with
toothed or wavy margins.
Care: It prefers a rich, well-drained
soil and a sunny position. Sow seeds
under glass in March covered with a
fine layer of soil and germinate at 50-
55F for about nine days. Prick out into
single 8 cm pots and continue growing at the same temperature until
April. Harden off in a cold frame and
plant out in May 30 cm apart. Can be
sown direct in April and thinned out.
Uses: Leaves can be picked young and
boiled or braised as with spinach. Rich
in iron. Used largely, however, as an
ornamental plant.

BORAGO officinalis
Borage

Flowering period: May to August.
Colour: vivid blue(flowers).
Height: up to 60 cm.
A tall annual with hairy leaves which
keeps blooming for months whatever
the weather. It has been cultivated
since medieval times for its ability to
refresh and invigorate. It was added to
the stirrup cup of those leaving for the
crusades but nowadays finds its way
more often into Pimms.
Care: It is best grown from seed as it
does not transplant very well. It likes
light soil, which can be poor quality,
but needs a sunny, well-drained spot.
Long roots make it unsuitable for
container growing. Sow seeds 5 cm
deep and 60 cm apart, from spring to
summer, putting two or three at each
station and thinning to keep the
strongest. Plants are fully-grown in 5
to 6 weeks.
Uses: An infusion of leaves is used as
a tonic and for liver, kidney and constipation problems. Leaves and seeds
stimulate milk flow in nursing moth-
ers. Add chopped leaves to salads,
egg dishes, cheese and yoghurt for its
cucumber flavour.

CALENDULA officinalis
Marigold

Flowering period: June to October.
Colour: orange and yellow(flowers).
Height: 45-70 cm.
This hardy annual adds a magnificent splash of colour to your garden while serving a whole range of medical, cosmetic and culinary uses. It was once used for curing warts and though its effectiveness may be questioned it is sure to be more efficient at this than the method it replaced – running a snail through with a spike and hanging it in the woodshed.
Care: Sow seeds in spring and autumn in light soil in a sunny spot. Thin seedlings to 45 to 60 cm apart. Though an annual it will seed itself and come up year after year.
Uses: Fresh or dried leaves make a tea to help with gastro-intestinal problems like ulcers, cramps and diarrhoea. It will also help poor circulation and varicose veins. Oil from the flowers makes a sunburn ointment also useful for acne. Use the flower petals in a bath for tired limbs. Fresh petals can also be added sparingly to salads and used as a flavouring for rice, cheese and savoury dishes.

CARTHAMUS tinctorius
Safflower or Saffron thistle

Flowering period: June.
Colour: orange/red(flowers).
Height: up to 90 cm.
A hardy annual native to India but introduced into this country in 1551. It can be grown quite well in Britain and Northern Europe and is becoming a popular substitute for the enormously costly saffron. It does not have quite the right taste but is a fraction of the cost.
Care: It prefers a sunny border though initially it is best to grow it in a sheltered spot so sow seeds in March at $1/2$ cm deep and transfer to its flowering position in May.
Uses: As a substitute for saffron and as a source of safflower oil which is a good kitchen oil. The seeds and even the leaves of the plant are edible.

CARUM carvi
Caraway

Flowering period: May and June.
Colour: white or yellow(flowers).
Height: up to 60 cm.
A biennial or perennial plant grown mainly for its ripe seeds which spill from the ripened fruit. It is most commonly used in German and Austrian cooking especially in Sauerkraut and goulash and on bread and seed cake.
Care: Sow seeds in early summer or autumn in a light, well-drained soil and a sunny spot. Thin to 20 cm apart. When the fruit has turned brown, before it bursts open, remove the seed heads and dry indoors. When completely dry, rub the seeds from the stalks and put in an airtight screwtop jar.
Uses: The seeds, chewed or in a tea, aid digestion and appetite. Use a small amount of seeds to flavour pork and liver and vegetables like cabbage, cauliflower or potatoes. The seeds are also used in baking. Crushed seeds can be added to pot pourris.

CENTAURIUM minus
Centaury

Flowering period: June to September.
Colour: pink(flowers).
Height: 18-36 cm.
Essentially a maritime plant, this annual grows in many coastal areas though it is selective about sites it choses and mechanical workings and quarries have probably reduced its presence. It is said to have been used by Chiron the centaur to treat an arrow wound in his foot made by Hercules.
Care: Sow seeds shallowly in April in a cold frame or in very light soil. Plant in the flowering position when about 5 cm.
Uses: Fresh or dried flowers can be used in a tisane or tea which enlivens the appetite. In some parts of Europe it is used as a febrifuge or fever treatment in the same way as quinine.

CHELIDONIUM majus
Celandine

Flowering period: May.
Colour: yellow(flowers).
Height: 30-60 cm.
Nicknamed 'swallow-wort' because it was said to bloom when the swallows arrived this perennial herb of the poppy family has hairy stems and coarsely-toothed leaves. The latex is not only poisonous but bitter in flavour and protects the plant from destruction by animals. The plant disappears in winter. It is the only representative of its genus in the British flora and is usually found wild where there has been some form of human habitation.
Care: Propagate by root division at any time during the growing season.
Uses: The bitter juice yielded by this plant has been used as a remedy for ringworm but there are probably far better methods for this today. Wormwood is probably a better option. It is said to be a cure for warts and useful in treating jaundice.

CHRYSANTHEMUM parthenium
Feverfew

Flowering period: July to September.
Colour: white(flowers).
Height: 25-45 cm.
A hardy short-lived perennial with an unpleasant odour of stale chamomile, it used to be grown mainly for its decorative qualities but recent discoveries reveal significant uses in the treatment of migraine. Deeply indented greenish yellow foliage.
Care: Sow seeds in spring in a shady spot and it will establish itself readily. Self-seeding, it likes most types of soil though it prefers it to be well-drained.
Uses: In ancient times it was used for treating fever as its name suggests but this use fell out of favour until very recently when migraine sufferers started to chew the leaves. Research by the London Migraine Centre now shows that significant results can be obtained in this way. Active chemicals in the leaves appear to stop the blood vessels going into spasm – which is said to be a cause of migraine symptoms.

CICHORIUM intybus
Chicory

Flowering period: July to October.
Colour: sky blue(flowers).
Height: up to 90 cm.
A hardy perennial grown for the slightly bitter, hearted head used in spring and winter salads and as a decorative plant in herbaceous and mixed borders.
Care: If soil is not chalk or lime then top dress with carbonated lime in the spring. Sow seeds in late April or early May in 1¹/₂ cm drills 38 cm apart. Thin to 25 cm when the seedlings show the third leaf. In November when the leaves die down and the roots are fully-grown lift them carefully. They will be up to 36 cm long and 8 cm thick at the top. Trim to 20 cm long, cut off foliage above the crown and store in a frost-free cool place. Force a few roots at a time packing them upright in pots or boxes, 5-8 cm apart, in light sand or soil. Shut out all light and put in a temperature of 7-10 degreesC (45-50degrees F). Cut when hearts are 12-15 cm long.
Uses: Mainly in salads but the tap-roots can be used ground in coffee to give it extra bite and flavour.

COCHLEARIA armoracia
Horseradish

Flowering period: June and July (not every season).
Colour: white(flowers), dark green-(leaves).
Height: 60-100 cm.
Horseradish is thought to have been one of the bitter herbs eaten at the Passover feast. This perennial has been cultivated in Europe since the 12th century for its tap-root. This is scrubbed clean and any discoloured bits cut off before use.
Care: It can be propagated annually from cuttings taken in the autumn. These should be placed in sand boxes in a cool, dark place. In early spring seedlings should be planted out in well-drained soil which has been deeply dug so that the roots can grow long and straight. Thin out to 30 cm apart. Bury roots, large end upwards, 5 cm deep. Harvest roots in October.
Uses: It is mainly used to make horse-radish sauce which is superb with beef or oily or smoked fish. Horseradish is also used in embrocations for chilblains and stiff muscles.

CONVALLARIA majalis
Lily of the Valley

Flowering period: April and May.
Colour: white(flowers).
Height: 15-20 cm.
A hardy herbaceous perennial which flourishes in woods and shady places. Sweetly-perfumed it has pale-green leaves which grow in pairs, and arching stems which carry between five and eight waxy, bell-shaped flowers. Over the centuries it has become associated with the spring festivals and is regarded as a symbol of regeneration and a return to happiness.
Care: Grow in partial shade in any ordinary garden soil. Plant crowns singly in September or October about 8-10 cm apart with the pointed end just below the surface. To propagate divide between October and March. Sow seeds when ripe, and before October, in boxes of seed compost. Transfer to a seed bed and nurture for three years before planting on.
Uses: A digitalis like drug that acts similarly on the heart is produced by this plant and is richest during the flowering period.

CORIANDRUM sativum
Coriander

Flowering period: June to August.
Colour: white or pinkish mauve(flowers).
Height: up to 60 cm.
An annual spice herb grown mainly for the culinary uses of its aromatic seeds. It is best grown out of doors because until the seeds ripen it has an unpleasant smell.
Care: Sow seeds early in spring in a light, rich soil in full sun. Thin to 10-15 cm apart. Coriander needs as long a growing season as possible for the seeds to ripen. When they have turned light, greyish-brown, cut the plants down and dry them in an airy place for two or three days. Shake out the seeds and store them in a screw-top jar.
Uses: The ground seeds are an important part of curry powder and spice mixtures and the green herb is used in all Asian cooking. An infusion of seeds is used to help digestion and relieve flatulence and crushed seeds are used in rubbing alcohol for a skin freshener.

CROCUS sativus
Saffron crocus

Flowering period: September to
November.
Colour: violet(flowers).
Height: up to 10 cm.
Saffron comes from the stigmas of the
saffron crocus and it has been famous
for centuries as a dye, perfume,
medicament and seasoning. It is,
however, tremendously costly to grow
because in the first year of cultivation
one hectare yields only 6 kg of dried
saffron. Each crocus has only three
stigmas and it needs 220.000 stigmas
to make half a kilogram. Clearly it also
requires enormous manpower to
harvest.
Care: It is not easy to grow in Britain or
Northern Europe because it needs a
long, hot summer to ripen its corms,
though Saffron Walden in England
took its name from the old saffron
industry there. Impractical and uneco-
nomic to grow in the domestic garden,
it is beginning to be replaced by
cheaper substitutes like the flowers of
the Safflower (Carthamus tinctorius)
See page 44.

CUMINUM cyminum
Cumin

Flowering period: June and July.
Colour: pink or white(flowers) deep
green(leaves).
Height: 30-60 cm.
An annual strongly resembling fennel
in leaf and character but grown for its
seed which is aromatic with a strong
warm taste. Used by the Romans as a
pepper substitute it is nowadays
mainly used in Indian, Middle Eastern
and Mexican cooking.
Care: Sow seeds in rich soil early in
the spring in full sun where it is to
flower. Thin plants to 15 cm apart.
After 3 or 4 months, if there has been
plenty of sunshine, the seeds should
be ready to harvest. Cut down the
plants and dry them indoors. Beware –
the seeds have an unpleasant flavour
when not fully ripe.
Uses: Ground seed is added to curry
powder or to dishes individually or
with a combination of other aromatic
spices. Whole seeds are used in rye
bread, pickles and chutney. An infusion of the seeds aids digestion.

EUPHORBIA lathyrus
Caper Spurge

Flowering period: July.
Colour: greenish-yellow(flowers).
Height: 50-70 cm.
A biennial plant which likes deep shade and moist soil. It is from a family of plants which includes castor oil, rubber and cassava. Many spurges contain a white milky latex which is highly poisonous and that of Caper spurge is harmful to the eyes.
In days gone by the seeds used to be picked and pickled but nowadays, if it is grown, it is largely a decorative plant.
Care: It grows well in ordinary garden soil in sun or partial shade. Sow seeds in March or April and thin out to 45 cm.
It can be propagated from young 8-10 cm shoots taken in April or May, dipped in powdered charcoal and planted singly in peat and sand equally mixed. Keep at a temperature of 18-21C (64-70F) and pot on.
Uses: It is said that the roots of the mature plant secrete a substance disliked by moles. Attractive in a wild garden.

FILIPENDULA ulmaria
Meadow Sweet

Flowering period: June to September.
Colour: creamy white(flowers).
Height: 90-120 cm.
A perennial plant which chooses woods, fens, river banks and other damp places as its home. It blossoms throughout summer and smells strongly of almonds. It is a useful herb, not only for its medical applications but because it is a plant which will grow and flourish in damp places where some others might not. Its heavy, soporific aroma led to the belief that it was associated with death.
Care: Since it likes damp, waterside conditions find as damp a garden spot as you can. Propagate by root division of its sturdy rhizomes.
Uses: Flowering tips can be removed and used in a tisane for relieving a head cold. Its action is slightly binding and an infusion can be used in the treatment of diarrhoea and colic.

FOENICULUM vulgare
Fennel

Flowering period: July to October.
Colour: bright yellow(flowers).
Height: up to 1.5 metres.
This biennial or perennial plant has a
flavour similar to anise. Both leaves
and seeds are important in cooking.
Its flowers come in large compound
umbels and its yellowish-brown seeds
are oval and ribbed. Gladiators are
said to have been garlanded with it
before entering the arena.
Care: It is easily grown from seed and
can withstand most conditions though
it prefers moist, well-drained soil and
a sunny spot. Sow seed in early spring
and thin to 30 cm apart. Self-sown
seedlings appear freely but main
plants can be divided every 3 to 4
years. Harvest seeds when hard and
grey-green. Cut off heads and dry
indoors.
Uses: Known as the 'fish herb' its uses
mainly relate to the cooking of fish.
Add seeds to water when cooking and
use chopped leaves in fish sauces.
Use seeds whole or ground on bread,
biscuits and soups. An infusion of
seeds is used for tired eyes and fennel
tea is used as a diuretic and laxative.

GAULTHERIA procumbens
Wintergreen

Flowering period: July and August.
Colour: white or pink(flowers).
Height: 7-15 cm.
Sometimes known as partridge-berry
because of its red berries, this small
evergreen creeping plant is hardy in
Britain and Europe and provides an all-
year interest in the rock garden or herb
garden.
Care: It likes moist, acid soil with peat
or lime-free mould. Plant in September, October or in April and May, in
partial shade away from drips of
overhanging trees. Can be propagated
by cuttings taken when 5-7 cm long
from lateral shoots, preferably with a
heel, in July or August. Put the rooted
cuttings in a cold frame into which you
have put peat and sand in equal parts
by volume. Pot the cuttings the following spring. Place outdoors until the
autumn when they should be planted
on.
Uses: The leaves are sharply astringent and aromatic because of their oil
– oil of wintergreen – which, when
made into an ointment, is used as an
embrocation to alleviate stiffness,
swellings and rheumatism.

GENTIANA lutea
Yellow Gentian

Flowering period: July and August.
Colour: yellow(flowers).
Height: 90-150 cm.
A hardy perennial which is by far the most important of the numerous gentians. Commonly found in damp meadows of the lower Alps it has mid-green, markedly veined leaves, long yellow flowers and was grown for centuries because of its reputed medical qualities. Herbalist Gerard called it 'fellwort' because it was said to cure whitlows or felons.
Care: May be raised from seed sown in compost before October and placed in a cold-frame. Prick out and plant in September in a sunny position. Likes partial shade. May also be propagated by root division in March.
Uses: Its large spongy root produces gentian bitter, or jenzmer, which is used as an effective non-astringent tonic and usually drunk with lemon or orange peel.

GERANIUM robertianum
Herb Robert

Flowering period: May to September.
Colour: pink(flowers).
Height: up to 45 cm.
Recognised as a member of the gera-nium family by its long-beaked seed case this plant was probably named after the 11th century French saint Robert, Abbot of Molerne whose medical skills were legendary. Com-mon in lightly-shaded places its divided leaves with reddish bases give off a powerful scent which accounts for its nickname 'Stinking Bob'.
Care: A straggling but dainty plant seldom cultivated and rarely found in a seed packet. Propagate by division between September and March and replant in the flowering position.
Uses: The flowers can be made into a mouthwash for ulcers and can also be pulped and used to stem the flow of blood on cuts. An infusion of the leaves can be taken for gout. Its powerful odour can be used in insecti-cides especially for the bedding of animals.

GLECHOMA hederacea
Ground Ivy

Flowering period: April to September.
Colour: blue, purple, pink or white(flowers).
Height: 10-30 cm.
A ground-hugging perennial, long used all over Europe to clarify beer and give it flavour, this herb was superseded by hops and was later used, instead, as a tisane or tea in the markets of Elizabethan England.
Care: Since it can be found almost anywhere wild it is not often cultivated. Young stems with leaves and flowers are cut off near the ground in April, May or July.
Uses: The scent is aromatic and the taste bitter and spicy so it is used mainly for seasoning in soups, egg dishes, stuffings and herbal cheeses. When dried it should be stored in a tight jar and can be used in an eye lotion and as a tea for headaches and to soothe nerve disorders.

GLYCYRRHIZA glabra
Liquorice

Flowering period: June and July.
Colour: bluish purple(flowers).
Height: 1-2 metres.
A perennial plant originally from the Mediterranean it is grown for its bright yellow, sweet, root. Once cultivated in the English county of Yorkshire near Pontefract it established the town as the centre of liquorice making in England.
Care: Deep, crumbly, stone-free soil is needed and it must be cultivated at least to a depth of 75 cm to allow straight roots. Plant root pieces 6-8 cm long, with eyes, in March or April at a depth of 4-6 cm then pray for a warm, dry spring. Shoots should be cut down to soil level each November for the first two years. In the third year, in the autumn, roots can be lifted.
Uses: Black liquorice is made by boiling the root with water and is used only in sweets. Liquorice has an antispasmodic effect and helps an upset stomach. It also has diuretic qualities and is used in the treatment of duodenal ulcers. Taken for too long it leads to the retention of water in the body.

HELICHRYSUM angustifolium
Curry plant

Flowering period: July and August.
Colour: yellow(flowers).
Height: up to 40 cm.
A perennial native to the Mediterranean regions, it is so-called because of the smell rather than its use. It is grown mainly for its rather attractive silver-grey foliage.
Care: It will thrive in any ordinary well-drained soil in a sunny spot. Plant outdoors between August and September or April and May, in sheltered positions, preferably at the base of a south-facing wall. In severe winters protect it by placing straw or bracken around the roots. It can be propagated by cuttings or lateral shoots 7 cm long, preferably with a heel, taken in July and August. Insert in a rooting mixture of three parts coarse sand and one part peat and pot into 7-8 cm containers. Overwinter in a cold frame and pot on into 10-12 cm pots the following May. Place outdoors until transplanting in August or September.
Uses: Mainly decorative in the curry plant can be hung up in bunches to use as a moth repellant or to keep away musty smells.

HUMULUS lupulus
Hop

Flowering period: autumn.
Colour: yellowish green(flowers).
Height: up to 6 metres.
This vigorous perennial vine belongs to the same family as hemp (cannabis) and is cultivated largely for the production of beer, though the Romans used the shoots as vegetables. Hops give ale its refreshing, slightly bitter taste.
Care: Hop plants must have support so sow in late spring in rich, well-dug, soil in full sun against a fence or wall. Thin seedlings to 15 cm apart and water well in dry weather. Also propagate by root division in spring. Gather female flowers for drying in early autumn and cut down plants later that month.
Uses: Apart from in brewing hops are used mostly for their calming effect on the nervous system. Hop tea is used for nervous diarrhoea, insomnia and restlessness. Hop leaves can also be used together with other leafy vegetables in a summer soup. They lose their effectiveness quickly when stored.

HYPERICUM perforatum
St John's Wort

Flowering period: July.
Colour: yellow(flowers).
Height: 30 cm.
Associated with the Knights of St John
during the Crusades it was commonly
used to heal open wounds inflicted
during the battles. In days gone by it
was also hung around the home
because it was believed this would
ward off evil spirits.
Care: It will practically grow with no
care at all once planted in light, rich
soil to which a little peat or leaf mould
has been added. Propagate by division
in March or by seeds sown in early
summer. It prefers to be planted in
shady areas of your herb garden or
border.
Uses: A soothing oil made from the
herb using the stems, leaves or flowers can be applied to cuts and abra-
sions. It can also be used to relieve eye
inflammations and styes. The oil also
soothes the pain of burns. Like most
bitter herbs it stimulates the action of
the kidneys and is therefore a diuretic.

HYSSOPUS officinalis
Hyssop

Flowering period: June to October.
Colour: bluish purple or deep pink(flowers).
Height: up to 60 cm.
This is a hardy evergreen perennial
introduced into Central Europe in the
10th century by Benedictine monks
and used as an ingredient of liquers
like Chartreuse. Popular with bees and
butterflies it adds an old world charm
to your herb garden.
Care: Sow seeds in the spring in light,
well-drained, soil in a sunny position.
Thin to 60 cm apart. It may also be
propagated from stem cuttings in the
spring or container grown. Once
established hyssop seeds itself. Kept
clipped it also makes a neat, useful
hedge plant.
Uses: Hyssop tea is drunk for catarrh,
colds and chest problems. Boiled
leaves can be used as a wash for burns
and bruises. Its faintly minty taste
gives a tang to green salads and
soups. It can also be used in making
perfumes and pot pourris.

IMPATIENS balsamina
Balsam

Flowering period: June to September.
Colour: pink(flowers), pale-
green(leaves).
Height: up to 75 cm.
A half-hardy annual which, because of
its compact size, is suitable for growing either in pots or beds. Parent to
several named varieties including
pink, white, crimson and purple
forms, it has lanceolate (lance-
shaped) leaves and the pink flowers,
about 3¹/₂ cm wide, appear in the
upper leaf axils from June to September.
Care: Sow seeds in pots of seed
compost in March at a temperature of
16-18 degrees C (61-64 degrees F).
Prick out the seedlings when large
enough to handle and place in containers of potting compost if they are to
be grown as pot plants. Otherwise
harden off the plants and place them in
the flowering site outside in late May.
Grow in ordinary soil, well-drained
and fertile, in full sun or partial shade.
Uses: Inhaling the steam from balsam
and boiling water is one of the oldest
ways of aiding breathing and blocked
noses.

INULA helenium
Elecampane

Flowering period: August and September.
Colour: bright yellow(flowers).
Height: 90-120 cm.
Formerly known as Enula or Scabwort
this coarse-leaved hardy herbaceous
perennial is a member of the daisy
family and has served man since
Roman times. Its name derives from
Helen, the wife of Menelaus, who it is
said gathered a bunch of the herb
when carried away by Paris. It later
saw use by veterinarians as a horse
medicine and in healing sheep scab.
Care: Inulas should be planted from
October to March in a moisture retaining spot. The soil should be fertile and
the location sunny. Propagate by
division between March and October.
Uses: The leaves are bitter, though
aromatic, and as the basis of a sweet it
is sucked to relieve asthma. Boiling up
the root creates a general tonic which
aids digestion. A cordial can be made
by infusing the roots with wine, port or
honey.

IRIS florentina
Orris

Flowering period: May.
Colour: bluish-white(flowers).
Height: 60-90 cm.
A bearded iris, native to the Mediterranean, whose finely-ground root provides orris powder which is the classic basis for pot pourris and pomanders. It was once commonly used in sixteenth century kitchens as a culinary herb and at one time the juice, mixed with wine, was given in treating dropsy. Nowadays its uses are largely connected with perfume though it does appear in some unusual liquers.
Care: Easy to grow provided it is given a sunny, well-drained spot. Propagate by root division at almost any time and especially in late spring and early summer. Ensure that the crowns are exposed and allowed to bask in sunlight.
Uses: The dried powder can be used in snuff to clear the head and a pinch of powder in washing water gives clothes a fresh smell. Mainly, however, it is used in pot pourris because it has a splendid fragrance and it absorbs moisture.

IRIS pseudacorus
Yellow Flag Iris

Flowering period: June.
Colour: golden yellow(flowers).
Height: 90-120 cm.
This perennial plant covers many water meadows, river banks and canals and for hundreds of years has been used as a dye plant. Known also as Fleur de Lis it has been adopted as the emblem of kings and conquerors throughout history.
Care: Easily cultivated, the yellow flag iris likes well prepared, water retentive, soil on the fringes of a pond or boggy patch. It is also suitable for a garden pond or pool. Plant in March or April, or in August and September, in full sun. If planting in water, up to a depth of 45 cm. Propagate by dividing rhizomes immediately after flowering or at any time when there is no active growth. Re-plant immediately. It can also be easily raised from seed sown in March or April. Stand seed boxes in partial shade, prick out singly into 8 cm pots and plant in the flowering site in September.
Uses: The rhizomes produce a black ink dye and the flowers a yellow one.

JUNIPERUS communis
Juniper

Flowering period: April and May.
Colour: yellow or green(flowers).
Height: up to 4 metres.
A native of the chalk and limestone regions of Britain this evergreen shrublike conifer has long been cherished for its rejuvenating properties. Branches of the bush were once used for fumigating houses to ward off disease.
Care: It grows best in open, well-rained positions. Sow seeds in spring in a cold frame and plant out of doors a year later. It can also be grown from stem cuttings taken from new growth by setting in sandy soil under glass in autumn. Plant out the following spring. Place male and female plants next to one another to ensure berries. The male plant grows more upright. Pick berries in autumn and dry in thin layers in an airy place below 35 degrees C (95F) to keep their oils.
Uses: Crushed berries in stuffings and for pork and pates. Use for flavouring alcoholic drinks like gin and juniper brandy. Chew berries for indigestion and as a diuretic.

LAURUS nobilis
Bay

Flowering period: April and May.
Colour: creamy white(flowers).
Height: up to 15 metres.
A perennial evergreen tree originating in Asia Minor and cherished for its magical qualities in days gone by. It was used for the laurel victor's crown in Ancient Greece and Rome. Nowadays it is grown for its aromatic. leathery, shiny leaves.
Care: It is best grown from plants available at garden centres or from half-ripened shoot cuttings taken in July or August. Plant in ordinary soil in a sunny position but bring indoors during severe winters. Top dress occasionally with either manure or bone-meal. Pick leaves for use throughout the year.
Uses: Bay is an important ingredient in cooking providing one third of the classic bouquet garni and also a fundamental ingredient for marinades and to flavour meat and vegetables. Bay oil, pressed from leaves and berries, is used in ointments for skin complaints and rheumatism.

LAVANDULA officinalis
Lavender

Flowering period: June to August.
Colour: mauve or white(flowers).
Height: 30-90 cm.
A perennial shrub with many varieties
and species whose name comes from
the Latin 'lavandulus' meaning 'to be
washed'. Sprigs were thrown into
baths in ancient times to perfume the
water. It is still grown commercially
for its perfume.
Care: It can be grown from seed, root
division or from cuttings. Remove
cuttings from established plants with a
heel and set in sand in the summer. It
will have rooted by late autumn. Plant
in open ground the following spring, in
well-drained, lime soil in a sunny spot.
In severe winters protect it especially
from high winds.
Uses: Bags of lavender added to the
bath water make a refreshing tonic.
Lavender water is made with one part
flowers and four of rubbing alcohol,
left one month before straining. Dried
leaves in pot pourris and boiled leaves
are useful for stomach complaints. An
embrocation from the oil is used for
muscular stiffness.

LEVISTICUM officinalis
Lovage

Flowering period: June to August.
Colour: greenish yellow(flowers).
Height: up to 2 metres.
A vigorous hardy perennial cultivated
in Europe since the Middle Ages. Its
small pale flowers are followed by
oblong deep brown seeds. All parts of
the plant may be used and, since early
times, its cleansing and deodorizing
properties have made it popular in
bath additives.
Care: It can be cultivated by sowing
seeds in thick moist soil, in sun or
partial shade, thinning the drills to
60 cm. It will self-seed and self-sow,
thus continuing for several years.
Ensure the supply of leaves by cutting
off early flowers. It also propagates by
root division in spring.
Uses: It makes a warming hot tea that
is also a good diuretic and aids problems like ulcers and diarrhoea. Bathe
sore feet in an infusion of flower
petals. It is useful in soups, though
sparingly, and a few leaves added to
salads give them a refreshing bite.

LINUM usitatissimum
Common Flax

Flowering period: June and July.
Colour: pale blue(flowers).
Height: up to 60 cm.
A hardy annual now naturalised in Great Britain and Northern Europe. It has linear lanceolate (lance-shaped) leaves which are pale green. Its slender stems carry single saucer-shaped blue flowers 1$^1/_2$ cm across.
Care: Sow in the flowering site in September or March and thin out the seedlings to 12 cm apart. Grow in any ordinary, well-drained soil in an open spot. A growing site in full sun is very important if the full effect of its brilliant blue flowers is to be achieved. It may also be grown in pots to flower under glass.
Uses: Largely grown these days for its decorative qualities, flax has medicinal value too: the seed is laxative, and, used as a powder, can be applied in case of infection.

LIPPIA citriodora
Lemon verbena

Flowering period: July to September.
Colour: white or mauve(flowers).
Height: 1.5 metres.
A deciduous shrub grown generally for its lemon-scented leaves which are highly-prized for their use in teas and infusions. Native to Chile it arrived in Europe in the 18th century. It has a woody stem, long narrow pointed leaves and tiny flowers carried in pointed spikes. The leaves, unlike most other fragrant plants, hold their scent best if picked in August.
Care: Grown from stem cuttings taken from an established plant which can be planted at any time in the growing season in well-drained soil. It prefers a sheltered spot and, if grown outdoors, needs to be protected. Prune in February to within 30 cm of the base and to stop it becoming straggly in the growing season pinch out the tops of shoots.
Uses: Its strong lemon-flavoured leaves make a mild sedative tea. An infusion of leaves makes a relaxing bath and they are excellent dried in pot pourris. The leaves can also be used in herb pillows.

MAJORANA hortensis
Marjoram

Flowering period: July to October.
Colour: white or pink(flowers).
Height: up to 50 cm.
An annual, biennial or perennial herb whose branched stems bear ovate leaves. It is a fragrant, pale-grey and woolly plant with fruits that form nutlets. It was used by the Egyptians, Romans and Greeks mainly as a medicinal herb and for love potions. Its spicy scent and taste is preferred nowadays for cooking.
Care: The annual variety is best for cultivation and should be treated as a half-hardy plant. Sow seed early, in light rich soil under glass. Plant out 20 cm apart in early summer in a sheltered spot. It grows well indoors in containers.
Uses: It is especially good with meat dishes particularly meat-loaf and Italian sauces. It goes naturally with tomatoes, marrows, courgettes and sprinkled on pizzas. Use dried leaves in muslin to keep away moths. An infusion of leaves aids digestion and coughing and helps to relieve headaches and menstrual cramps.

MARRUBIUM vulgare
White Horehound

Flowering period: June to September.
Colour: white(flowers).
Height: 30-60 cm.
A perennial whose tiny white flowers are born in dense whorls. A British native plant it is common all over Europe and although untidy was once common in most cottage gardens where it was used in beer-making and, before that, because, as its name suggests, it was used as an antidote to the bite of raging dogs. It is one of the five bitter herbs of the Mishna which the Jewish people took during the Passover.
Care: It is propagated by stem cuttings. Plant in any soil but it prefers an open situation and is likely to grow in a somewhat ungainly fashion.
Uses: In Regency days the ground herb was often used in snuff because it has nasal clearing properties. It can be used in treating a variety of cold symptoms. To ease a painful hacking cough or a cold, use the leaves or flowers in an infusion. A tea, sweetened with honey is useful in treating chest congestion.

MATRICARIA chamomilla
Chamomile

Flowering period: July to August.
Colour: white(flowers).
Height: 40 cm.
An annual plant often referred to as
'true' chamomile and the one most
used for medicinal purposes. Still
most appreciated in other countries
and often confused with the Roman
chamomile (Anthemis nobilis) which
is more commonly used in making
lawns.
Care: Sow early in spring or autumn in
rows 20-30 cm apart. The very fine
seeds should be sown on a humid day,
mixed with sand, and watered gently
while they are germinating. It seeds
itself in successive years and will
appear all over your garden. Harvest
from May to October, eight weeks
after sowing and only when it is sunny.
Dry quickly and keep in an airtight
container.
Uses: Flowers of the 'true' chamomile
have a pleasant flavour and as an
infusion have a soothing action on the
digestive system. They can also be
used as a herbal rinse for fair hair.

MELITOTUS officinalis
Melilot

Flowering period: June to September.
Colour: yellow(flowers).
Height: up to 90 cm.
Once grown as a fodder crop, like
clover, it gives off an aroma very
similar to new-mown hay when dried.
The scent lasts some time because of
its coumarin content. The name
derives from 'mel' meaning 'honey'
and is meant as a tribute to its great
popularity with bees. A very sturdy
plant, it grows in conical shape and
has delicately textured bright green
foliage similar to laburnum.
Care: Seed collected from wild plants
in September or, if you are fortunate,
from a specialist herb dealer, can be
sown immediately. The plant is self-
seeding spilling its seeds from pods.
Uses: Scattered in clothes or linen, or
in moth bags, it works as an ideal
deterrent to moths and other insects.
It can be made into a tea or tisane to be
used as a treatment for flatulence and
other digestive problems.

MELISSA officinalis
Lemon Balm

Flowering period: July and August.
Colour: white, pink or blue(flowers).
Height: up to 90 cm.
A bushy perennial native to the Mediterranean but commonly found in most parts of Europe – often growing by the roadside. Hairy stem, light-green hairy leaves and small flowers growing in leaf axils. It was once used by apiarists to keep bees within their hives because of its attractiveness to them. Its name, in fact, derives from the Greek word 'melissa' meaning 'bee'. It was a sacred herb in the Temple of Diana.
Care: Slow to germinate, it can be sown in the spring for planting out in autumn. Harvest the leaves the following year. It is best grown from stem cuttings taken in spring or autumn and planted in damp soil in partial shade. Will need to be strongly cut-back since it spreads rapidly.
Uses: Use as a substitute for lemon in stuffings and cooking chicken. Can be added to fruit cups, ice-cream and salads. An infusion of leaves makes a relaxing tea.

MENTHA aquatica
Water Mint

Flowering period: August to September.
Colour: lilac(flowers).
Height: up to 60 cm.
A perennial plant and just one of the myriad varieties of mint. Select the ones you will most need. A native to the British Isles it thrives in fenland and soggy, wooded areas. Strongly-scented it is a rival to peppermint. Square, erect stem and opposite single green leaves it often takes on a reddish tinge.
Care: Mints are propagated by root division in spring or autumn. Roots should be laid horizontally 5 cm deep in April and May. In dry weather water well.
Uses: Cooks will have to decide which of the many varieties of mint they most favour since a great many of them have duplicate uses. Mint sauce, an ideal accompaniment to lamb, can be made with water mint or others. It also goes well with new potatoes, peas and carrots. An infusion of the leaves can be used to aid the digestion.

MENTHA citrata
Eau-de-cologne Mint

Flowering period: mid to late autumn.
Colour: mauve(flowers).
Height: up to 60 cm.
A fragrant perennial this mint has grown more popular because of its cologne scent and its use in drinks and pot pourris. It resembles water mint with its branched stems and egg-shaped, smooth, dull green leaves. It also has remarkable properties which enhance the fragrance of plants growing near it. Surface growing runners take on a splendid purple colour. Also known as Bergamot mint it was once placed in the baths of Ancient Greece for its smell and ability to refresh and revive.
Care: Plant rooted pieces of runners in spring or autumn in damp soil in sun or partial shade. Spreads rapidly and will need to be kept apart from other plants. Suitable for container growing.
Uses: Leaves for a facial steam, to clear the complexion and in face packs. Cooked with soups, peas, potatoes and in water ices.

MENTHA gentilis
Ginger Mint

Flowering period: July to September.
Colour: pale purple(flowers).
Height: up to 45 cm.
A hardy garden hybrid with reddish-purple stems and ovate lanceolate (lance-shaped) mid-green leaves. Pale purple flowers are carried in spikes which are 10-15 cm long from July to September. More of an ornamental plant than many mints this variety has the sort of foliage that makes it ideal for borders, rock gardens or between paving. Splashes of red, green and purple will give your garden a splendid, colourful show.
Care: It will grow in almost any type of soil but, like many mints, it really prefers a soil that does not dry out in summer. Plant in a sunny spot, or in partial shade, at any time from October to March. It is a very rapid-spreading plant and will need to be kept under control. Place roofing slates into the soil all around the plant. Propagate by divison at any time between October and March.
Uses: As with Water Mint.

MENTHA piperita
Peppermint

Flowering period: July to September.
Colour: mauve or white(flowers).
Height: up to 60 cm.
A hardy perennial often labelled as a separate species but, nowadays, believed to be a hybrid between water mint and spearmint. It is used to provide an oil for both pharmaceutical and confectionary uses. It is widely cultivated in Europe for this oil which contains menthol.
It has an erect stem tinged with red and dark-green leaves which are oval and deeply-indented.
Care: Plant rooted pieces of the long, underground runners in spring or autumn when there is no danger of frost. It thrives in rich, moist soil and in open ground. It is best grown in some bottomless container because it will rapidly encroach on other plants. Keep well-watered and cut-back regularly.
Uses: Peppermint tea is commonly used for insomnia, stomach pains, toothache and nervous disorders.

MENTHA rotundifolia
Apple Mint

Flowering period: early to mid autumn.
Colour: white or pale mauve(flowers).
Height: up to 60 cm.
Also known as woolly mint because of its soft, variegated, woolly leaves which are about 2¹/₂ cm across, this perennial is native to Europe and is often found in ditches and waste ground and in damp soil. The flowers come in dense, interrupted spikes and combine both the fragrance and the taste of apples and mint.
Care: Like most mints it can be simply grown from rooted pieces of the long, underground runners in spring or autumn. Plant in sun or partial shade. Once again, this mint is a rapid grower and will need to be contained with roof slates or something similar. It can be grown in containers. Encourage fresh growth by regular cutting. Renew after 3-4 years.
Uses: Adds a delicious taste to fruits, fruit salad and water ice. Add leaves to wine cups, fruit drinks, tea and mint juleps.

MENTHA spicata
Spearmint

Flowering period: August to September.
Colour: mauve(flowers).
Height: up to 60 cm.
This perennial has an erect stem with stiff upright shoots, long narrow leaves and terminal, cylindrical spikes of flowers. It is native to Southern Europe and produces copious underground runners which spread rapidly. Small labiate flowers are followed by very small, round brown seeds. It resembles peppermint but has no leaf stalks.
Care: Plant rooted pieces of the rhizome or runner in spring or autumn. The plant likes light, moist rich soil in sun or partial shade but should grow well in most soil. A rapid spreader it needs to be contained. Suitable for container growth it needs to be well-watered. Cut regularly and renew every three or four years.
Uses: Use leaves in a facial steam, for the complexion, face packs and creams. A tea helps insomnia and nervous disorders. In cooking it goes well in mint sauce, spreads, dips and mint juleps.

MONARDA didyma
Bergamot

Flowering period: July to September.
Colour: scarlet(flowers).
Height: up to 90 cm.
Often called 'bee balm' because of its great popularity with bees, this perennial plant has as quare, hairy stem and oval serrated leaves. It provided an alternative from which patriotic Americans made tea during the period of the Boston Tea Party when they boycotted English tea. A beautiful, old fashioned plant it brings a minty smell and swarms of bees into your garden.
Care: Bergamot is partial to a rich soil which is as moist as possible. It can be propagated by root division. Keep it free from weeds, renew regularly and throw away dead centres. Grows well in containers if well watered. It can also be grown from stem cuttings taken in July.
Uses: It makes a soothing tea with a slightly sedative effect. Earwigs like the flowers so always wash before use. Dried leaves and flowers are used in pot pourris and chopped the leaves can be added to salads.

MYRRHIS odorata
Sweet Cicely

Flowering period: early to mid-spring.
Colour: white(flowers).
Height: up to 90 cm.
A tall, quite beautiful perennial plant which has many advantages in a garden since it is the last to disappear in winter and first to appear in spring. It grows wild in northern England and Scotland. It has a hollow, grooved stem with large, soft leaves and small white flowers. The fruit is long, ridged and black. There is no strong scent but a definite smell of anise is given off and it also tastes quite distinctively of this too.
Care: A rampant growing plant it gets bigger each year. Sow in early spring in moist soil and partial shade. Thin to 18 cm. Its large taproots grow deeper and it also self-sows so there is no need to divide or transplant. Stopping it will be the problem.
Uses: Sweet Cicely can be used in bouquets of culinary herbs and in salad dressings and soups. A tea made from the leaves, or seeds chewed, aids digestion.

NASTURTIUM officinalis
Watercress

Flowering period: late June to October.
Colour: white(flowers).
Height: 30-60 cm.
A hardy, aquatic perennial plant native to Europe and commercially cultivated in shallow tanks because of the fear that it might carry typhoid if grown in river water or stream water. Small rounded leaves grow on its branching stems and the tiny white flowers are followed by long, curved seed pods. In New Zealand it is regarded as a weed.
Care: It grows best in rich, sandy soil in clean running water. Can be sown in seed boxes in the early summer or autumn and planted out 15 cm apart. It can also be propagated by cuttings taken in spring or early autumn.
Uses: It is commonly used in fresh salads, soups and as a garnish with all foods. An infusion of watercress shoots is used to aid rheumatism, stomach upsets and catarrh. It is not to be taken for long periods.

NEPETA cataria
Catmint

Flowering period: May to September.
Colour: white(flowers).
Height: 60-80 cm.
A perennial plant beloved of cats but not very rewarding for any other purpose. It may be difficult to get it established in a garden since cats have a habit of rolling on young plants. Catnip tea used to be drunk in some quantity before the merciful arrival of Indian and China tea in Europe. It bears white flowers faintly marked with a bronze-red coloured dot and is natural to calcareous soils. It's also much loved by bees.
Care: It can be grown either from seed or by dividing its clusters of roots at any time in spring or early autumn. Though strictly a perennial it often behaves like a biennial, dying after it flowers.
Uses: Not simply, though mainly, to make your cat dopey with pleasure. It can also be used dried on pork. In the Middle Ages, it is said, the young shoots were used on salads and this habit survives in some parts of France still.

OCIMUM basilicum
Sweet basil

Flowering period: June to September.
Colour: white or pale red(flowers).
Height: 30-60 cm.
An annual plant native to India and one of the truly great culinary herbs despite the fact that the British Ministry of Agriculture has labelled it as 'of little or no importance'. Its hot, slightly clove-like flavour is prized in Italian dishes and though it may be difficult to grow it is worth persevering. Stems are bushy, branched and reddish while the leaves are long and dark green.
Care: It must either be grown from seed or bought as a pot plant. Sow in early summer in rich, light soil and a sheltered position. Plant out in summer 20 cm apart and when established pinch out to encourage healthy growth. Ideal for growing indoors. Don't overwater.
Uses: Provides the basis of many classic Italian sauces and goes with almost every tomato dish. Fresh leaves are used in salads, soups and with fish or veal. An infusion of the leaves is used for gastric problems and dried leaves as a snuff to clear noses.

ORIGANUM onites
Pot Marjoram

Flowering period: August to October.
Colour: white or pink(flowers).
Height: up to 60 cm.
A perennial plant native to the Mediterranean but now found wild in most of Europe. It's frequently grown because the preferable sweet marjoram (Majorana hortensis) is not hardy enough. Pot marjoram does not boast such a sweet flavour. Square, branched stems with hairy, small leaves and dense terminal clusters of flowers.
Care: Sow seeds early in the spring in well-drained, light soil in a sheltered spot. Seeds should be sown 1 cm deep and thinned to 25 cm. It can also be propagated by cuttings in early summer or root division in spring or autumn.
Uses: Marjoram is good with meat dishes though pot marjoram may not have quite the same taste. It should be used, perhaps, with more robust dishes which may also have garlic or wine with them. Dried leaves are used in moth bags.
Fresh leaves can make an infusion for digestive, cough and chest problems.

ORIGANUM vulgare
Wild Marjoram

Flowering period: August to October.
Colour: purple(flowers).
Height: up to 75 cm.
A pungent perennial herb native to Europe and the Middle East and grown commercially in the USA. Square stems with oval pointed leaves and purple, two-lipped flowers which come in terminal clusters. Technically it should be pungent all the time but if grown in cold or wet climates it may not be the herb of classic Neopolitan cooking but, instead, green and lacking in flavour. In Italy its flavour varies from town to town, indeed from field to field. In Mexico it is added to commercial chilli powder to give it that peppery flavour.
Care: Sow early in the spring in well-drained rich soil in a sheltered spot. Thin to 30 cm water in dry weather. Protect the roots in winter. Propagate by root division in spring or autumn.
Uses: Much stronger when grown in full sun and of all the marjorams the one which has the real peppery taste. Use dried in small quantities in spaghetti, pizza and other Italian dishes.

PAPAVER somniferum
Opium Poppy

Flowering period: June to August.
Colour: white, red or pink(flowers).
Height: up to 75 cm.
The oldest species of poppy in cultivation and an annual of great history and reputation. Known in the Mediterranean areas since medieval times and grown for a long time in the monasteries for its seeds – which carry no opiate. The use of this narcotic is said to have started on the trade routes to China by the Arabs in the 13th century. It became the scourge of China and in 1729 was prohibited by Emperor Yung Cheng – an act which led to the Opium Wars. A hardy species with deeply lobed, smooth pale grey-green leaves and flowers which are followed by bulbous, flat-capped seeds.
Care: Grown in ordinary soil, well-drained and sunny. Most will self-seed but if grown from seed do so in March, April or September. Propagate by division in March.
Uses: Seeds mostly used in confectionary on cakes and biscuits.

PETASITES hybridus
Butter Burr

Flowering period: January to March.
Colour: White or pink(flowers).
Height: 30 cm.
A small, hardy perennial plant which is useful in an herbaceous border or rock garden. It thrives with little care and has pink or white flowers born in long racemes. Its large leaves appear after the flower.
Care: It can be propagated by seeds sown in the summer or by division of the roots in November and February. Both methods are comparatively easy and will produce healthy flowers.
Uses: Largely used nowadays as a decorative border plant which has the advantage that it flowers from January to March at a time when most other plants carry no blooms. The fresh leaves however can be used for the outer treatment of wounds, and swallowed will act as a transpiration device.

PETROSELINUM crispum
Parsley

Flowering period: July to September.
Colour: yellow(flowers).
Height: up to 60 cm.
All the many varieties of parsley are
technically hardy biennials but are
usually treated as annuals because
this is both easier and the leaves are
crisper and tastier in the first year.
Since it is probably used in larger
quantities than any other herb large
clumps are needed. Rich in vitamins
A,B and C as well as various minerals
it is a health-giving plant which stimulates the digestion and improves the
working of the whole digestive system.
Care: It is not as tricky to grow as
many believe. Sow in late spring or
early summer in rich, moist soil and a
sheltered sunny spot. Seeds take a
while to germinate, up to 8 weeks, so
to help them along soak overnight in
water before sowing. Water well in dry
weather.
Uses: In almost all foods as a garnish
and flavouring. Chewed it removes the
smell of garlic. Parsley tea treats
coughs and asthma and is a general
tonic.

PIMPINELLA anisum
Anise

Flowering period: July or August.
Colour: white(flowers).
Height: up to 45 cm.
An annual plant which, rather like
coriander, has lobed leaves at the
base. It is difficult to grow because the
seeds for which it is mostly cultivated
need plenty of sun and only in a long
hot summer over here will they ripen
satisfactorily. A native of the Levant it
was used in ancient Egypt on sweets
and cakes. Perhaps it is most commonly used nowadays, however, in
strong alcoholic drinks of which most
Mediterranean countries have a versi-
on.
Care: Propagated by seed only. Sow in
light, well-drained soil in the early
summer. Thin to 15 cm and gather
seed-heads in early autumn. Complete
the drying indoors.
Uses: Leaves add flavour to salads and
seeds to biscuits and cakes. The seeds
are effective for many digestive problems when taken as a tea or simply
chewed. A face-pack made from
ground anise can be used to fade
freckles.

PLANTAGO major ruber
Plantain (Red)

Flowering period: June to October.
Colour: yellow-green(flowers).
Height: 10-45 cm.
An impressive perennial plant which was once known as 'weybread' because its roots were commonly used for baking. It has oblong, seven-veined leaves and thick, grooved stalks. A wild herb not cultivated in this country and considered by many to be no more than a weed. It can be found, however, in abundance in some parts of the countryside.
Care: Since you are unlikely to come across seeds or plants sold commercially the only way to grow plantain would be to find a clump growing wild and to take some roots and propagate by division. Do not, however, go about digging up the countryside with abandon.
Uses: Apply raw leaves to mosquito and other bites to ease the pain. An infusion of leaves is used to relieve coughs, diarrhoea and congestion. A poultice can be made which is applied to treat burns and bruises and chewing on the root is said to relieve pain.

POLYGONUM bistorta
Bistort

Flowering period: June to August.
Colour: pinkish red(flowers).
Height: up to 50 cm.
This perennial is often grown simply as a decorative plant and certainly its spiky pink flowers are impressive. Its early maturing leaves make it a significant feature of some landscapes where it grows wild and really stands out when little else is showing. The name derives from the Greek 'polys' meaning 'many' and 'gonu' meaning joint and refers to its zigzag stem pattern. Originally it was recommended as a treatment for debility and tuberculosis but nowadays it has a number of more realistic uses.
Care: Its true species is rarely cultivated but the variety 'superbum' is an excellent form which really makes the most of its colour. Plant between October and March in rich, moist soil and partial shade. Propagate by division in October and March.
Uses: As an astringent in cosmetic treatments or used sparingly in salads. Best, perhaps, treated as a truly decorative herb and planted with an eye to colour.

PORTULACA oleracea
Purslane

Flowering period: late summer.
Colour: yellow(flowers).
Height: up to 15 cm.
A pretty, tender annual not native to Europe but grown commercially in some countries, like the Netherlands, for a salad crop. It has succulent leaves and erect, reddish stems and the yellow flowers make it an attractive garden herb. In conjunction with sorrel if forms the flavoursome basis for the classic French soup dish bonne femme.
Care: Not to be sown with the slightest risk of frost. Sow in sandy soil and a sunny spot and thin to 10 cm. A quick germinator, the leaves will probably be ready for picking after about six weeks.
Uses: Most used as a salad herb it is added in small quantities, chopped, to green salads. Its thick mid-ribs or stems are sometimes pickled in vinegar for winter eating. An infusion of leaves can be taken for a tonic or laxative. It is rich in Vitamin C.
Fresh leaves can make an infusion for digestive, cough and chest problems.

PRIMULA veris
Cowslip

Flowering period: spring.
Colour: yellow(flowers).
Height: up to 30 cm.
Now regarded by many as a mere roadside weed this delightful spring-flowering plant is dying out because of modern agricultural methods and the disappearance of natural meadowland. Its wrinkled leaves form a loose rosette and its firm, pale green stems carry a cluster of yellow bells. It has a delicate, sweet scent and was used, many years ago, for making both wine and tea. It is said to be a soporific.
Care: Seeds would only be available from a specialist and should be sown out in April. These may produce inferior plants. It likes a shady position in any ordinary garden soil. Keep roots moist. Can be propagated by division in October or March.
Uses: Can be used to make an ointment, cream or toilet water to remove spots and wrinkles and treat sunburn. Not longer easy to find enough to make wine.
Fresh leaves can make an infusion for digestive, cough and chest problems.

PULMONARIA officinalis
Lungwort

Flowering period: April or May.
Colour: purple-blue(flowers).
Height: up to 30 cm.
A hardy, herbaceous perennial named because of its use as a medicinal herb centuries ago. It contains juices which are effective in treating pulmonary congestion but rarely used for this nowadays. Early herbalist Culpeper said it was good only for 'broken-winded horses'. It has narrow, elipti-cal, white-spotted leaves which account for its nickname 'spotted Mary'.
Care: Plant in October to March in a shady position. It should grow in almost any garden soil but try keeping the roots moist in dry weather either by mulching or by frequent watering. Propagate by division in October or March.
Uses: An infusion of the leaves, gathered early or in mid-season is used in the treatment of whooping cough or cold.

RHEUM officinalis
Medicinal Rhubarb

Flowering period: May.
Colour: yellow(flowers).
Height: 60-90 cm.
Medical rhubarb is among the oldest plants known to man and was written about in the Chinese herbal Pen-King which is believed to date from 2, 700BC. For some reason, however, it did not appear in western Europe until very many years later. It is considered to be a native of Tibet and came to us via France thanks to the French consul at Hankow. The root of the plant was one of the ingredients of the revolting Gregory's Powder, infamous among those forced to take it for stomach ailments, made also with magnesia and ginger.
Care: Plant from November to February in ordinary garden soil in a sunny spot. Water freely during dry spells. Leave the crowns undisturbed for at least three years then pick, wash, peel and dry. Can be propagated by division between November and February.
Uses: Mainly as a purgative and as a stimulus to the digestive tract. Useful for clearing the system of an unsatisfactory diet.

ROSA canina
Dog Rose

Flowering period: summer.
Colour: pink or white(flowers).
Height: up to 3 metres.
A wild climbing perennial shrub which produces the most sweet-smelling flower in summer. In the autumn the flowers are followed by shining red rose hips. Native to Europe it was used for centuries as a food and nowadays is largely grown for the perfume and the hips which provide a valuable source of vitamin C. Do not bring the hips into contact with any form of metal except stainless steel because this robs them of colour and vitamins.
Care: Although found wild and cultivated normally as hybrids they can be grown from cuttings taken in early spring or late autumn. Plant in rich, well drained soil in the sun. Best grown against a fence or trellis. Gather rose petals in summer and the hips after the first frost.
Uses: The petals, when dried, form the basis of pot pourris. The hips make wine, jelly, syrup or a tea which is a mild diuretic.

ROSMARINUS officinalis
Rosemary

Flowering period: May and June.
Colour: pale blue(flowers).
Height: up to 2 metres.
A marvellous sweet-smelling evergreen shrub with a host of uses. It grows very high but is also slow-growing. Short narrow leaves, tough and densely set. Little clusters of flowers in leaf axils. A symbol of fidelity, folklore claims that it variously stimulates the brain and aids the memory.
Care: It thrives in hot sun and poor soil provided it is well-drained and has some lime in it. Can be grown from seed but this is laborious. Either buy a plant or take stem cuttings in August and transplant in the spring. Can be container grown but may need to be brought indoors in winter.
Uses: In cooking its associations with lamb blind some people to other uses especially with meats, fleshy fish and in jams and jellies. An infusion aids digestion and stimulates the circulation. As a herbal hair rinse it will deepen the colour of dark hair. Fresh leaves can make an infusion for digestive, cough and chest problems.

RUMEX acetosa
Sorrel

Flowering period: summer.
Colour: red-green(flowers).
Height: up to 45 cm.
A hardy perennial herb quite common in most of Europe. Erect and graceful it has fleshy mid-green leaves which are arrow-shaped and flowers carried in narrow pyramid shapes. Nicknamed 'cuckoo's meat' it was said that the herb was eaten by cuckoos to strenthen their voices. It has sharp, acid-tasting leaves which contain tartaric acid and potassium salt and the juices act on milk in the same way as rennet.
Care: Sorrel will grow in well-drained and fertile soil in full sun or partial shade. Propagate by division in March, April or September and replant into growing position. Seeds can be sown in drills 45 cm apart. Thin to 8 cm.
Uses: Use the leaves in soups and a sauce to go with fish. A decoction of the root is used as a diuretic, for diarrhoea and for excessive menstruation. Use the leaves in a poultice or infusion for acne and skin problems.

RUTA graveolens
Rue

Flowering period: June and July.
Colour: yellow(flowers).
Height: up to 60 cm.
A hardy evergreen perennial probably introduced into Europe by the Romans who swore by its use for eye problems and even claimed that it gave second sight. More recently, however, it has been grown for use in treating abnormal blood pressure. A neat and tidy shrub it has ovate, deeply divided bluish-green leaves that give off a faintly acrid aroma. In June or July it produces stiff, almost sulphurous flowers.
Care: Sow seeds in March or April in compost and put in cold frame. Prick out seedlings and place in 8 cm pots. Harden, and plant in growing position in September, in a well-drained sunny position. Propagate by stem cuttings in August. Cut back in April to preserve its bushy shape.
Uses: A tea from the fresh leaves, well-sweetened, is taken for abnormal blood pressure. It is a stimulant. It is also used in the fiery Italian grape spirit grappa.

SALVIA officinalis
Sage

Flowering period: mid-summer.
Colour: purple(leaves).
Height: 30-45 cm.
A small evergreen shrub with a powerful flavour especially when grown in
hot and dry areas. Associated with
strength since ancient times it is native
to southern Europe especially the
Mediterranean. Woody at the base it
has oblong, slightly dusty-looking
leaves which are usually pale-grey. All
sage tends to look tired and old after
four or five years and it is best to
replace them.
Care: Grow in any soil that is well-
drained and sunny. Sow seed in the
early spring under glass and transplant in late spring or grow from stem
cuttings taken in late spring and plant
straight out. Pinch out the growing
tips to keep it bushy.
Uses: Most used in stuffings and with
pork but it can also be used in soups,
stews and, sparingly, in salads. Sage
tea is said to reduce perspiration and
help nervous conditions. Use the tea
also as a gargle for sore throats. Apply
crushed leaves to insect bites.

SAMBUCUS nigra
Elder

Flowering period: May to July.
Colour: creamy-white(flowers).
Height: up to 7 metres.
A hardy deciduous shrub with tough
straight-growing branches and a
creamy-white blossom known as
elder-flower which grows in clusters
giving a heady scent. The fruit, known
as elderberries, are usually ripe by the
end of summer. Blackbirds are especially partial to them. Cultivated centuries ago to ward off evil spirits and
witches.
Care: Very slow to get started from
seed so better to grow from young
plants in late autumn or early spring.
Take cuttings of leafless shoots in the
autumn and plant in good garden soil
in the sun or partial shade.
Uses: The elderflower makes a heady
wine and so too does the berry,
though this is rich in tannin and will
need to be laid down for two or three
years. Berries also make jams and
jellies. Hot elderflower tea makes a
soothing nightcap and elderberry
syrup relieves coughs and cold. A
lotion from the flowers makes a refreshing bath.

SANTOLINA chamaecyparissus
Cotton Lavender

Flowering period: July and August.
Colour: yellow(flowers).
Height: 30-60 cm.
A marvellous perennial plant whose
silver-grey foliage makes it worth
growing regardless of other uses. In
Tudor times it was commonly found as
an edging plant around herb gardens.
It enjoys regular close-clipping.
Preserve the silver effect if you wish by
cutting away the tiny button-like
yellow flowers.
Care: It thrives in full sun and almost
any soil which is well-drained. Plant in
September and October, March or
April. Propagate by stem cuttings
taken in July or September and place
in 8 cm pots of potting compost.
Harden outdoors before placing in
growing position in September. Cut to
shape periodically in summer and
prune hard into the old wood after
flowering.
Uses: Its aromatic leaves make an
ideal base for pot pourris and when
dried can be used in moth bags.

SAPONARIA officinalis
Soapwort

Flowering period: July to September.
Colour: pink(flowers).
Height: 30-90 cm.
A hardy perennial probably introduced
by the Romans who used it for water-
softening. When agitated in water its
leaves produce suds and it's a natural
detergent. Hence the name. Single-
pink flowers, pale-green, elliptical to
lance-shaped leaves. Invasive in some
gardens creeping rapidly along stout
rhizomatous roots.
Care: Grows happily in most soil in
sun or partial shade. Plant in good
weather in October or March. Propagate by division and replant at any
time. It can be sown by seed but this is
unreliable. Cut back strongly after
flowering for second crop of blooms.
Uses: Leaves make a cleansing lotion
for all skin. An infusion of leaves
makes a herbal shampoo. In olden
days the crushed leaves were used in a
decoction to treat bumps and bruises.
It is a natural detergent.

SATUREJA hortensis
Summer Savory

Flowering period: July to October.
Colour: pink or white(flowers).
Height: up to 40 cm.
A bushy, low-growing annual popular with Greeks and Romans for cooking. Erect stems becoming purple with age and long narrow leaves with two-lipped, small, dainty flowers. An aromatic plant good for the digestive system. If a leaf is boiled in the water with Brussel sprouts or cabbage the unpleasant smell normally given off will be reduced or eradicated.
Care: Sow seeds in light, rich soil in a sunny spot in drills. Thin to 15 cm. Can also be grown under glass in early spring and then transplanted but does not take kindly to being moved. Propagate by root division in spring or autumn and by stem cuttings in early summer.
Uses: An infusion of leaves for the digestion, to stimulate appetite or as a gargle for sore throats. As a seasoning use in meat, fish or egg dishes; add to wine vinegar.

SINAPSIS alba
White Mustard

Flowering period: May to July.
Colour: yellow(flowers).
Height: up to 1 metre.
An herbaceous annual usually grown in conjunction with cress (Lepidium sativum) and used in salads and sandwiches in the seedling stage. Commercially, rape seed is substituted for its more pungent taste. Commonly used in English and American mustard but forbidden in French Dijon mustard. Pungency comes from essential oils which form when crushed seeds are mixed with water.
Care: Most successfully grown under glass. Sow in very fine soil or compost or on moisture retaining material like cotton wool. Spread seeds thickly on top of growing medium, press down lightly, water and cover with black polythene. Place in a cold frame or in winter in a temperature of 7C (45F). When seeds have germinated remove from tray and eat.
Uses: In salads, sandwiches and on meat.

SOLIDAGO virgaurea
Goldenrod

Flowering period: August to October.
Colour: golden(flowers).
Height: 90-180 cm.
This hardy, herbaceous perennial was for centuries thought to mark the spot where buried treasure could be found. Instead the treasure lies in the literally glowing golden colour and the fact that it is often the last summer plant to remain in bloom. In the hands of a dowser it is said to be effective in detecting hidden springs.
Care: Found widely in woods, on banks and among rocks and since it is hardy will grow well almost anywhere. This virtue makes it useful for planting in rough areas of the garden. Propagate by root division in autumn or spring. Apt to impoverish the soil, so beware!
Uses: In a tea the leaves treat inflammation of the bladder and kidney and are mildly diuretic. Used as a disinfectant in Switzerland and sometimes used to staunch the flow of blood.

STACHYS officinalis
Betony

Flowering period: August to September.
Colour: purple(flowers).
Height: 45-75 cm.
A course, hardy perennial native to open woodland and heaths all over Europe. Its generic name 'stachys' comes from the Greek meaning 'spike' or 'ear' and relates to its terminal spikes which carry the bright purple flowers. Grown in monasteries once to treat short-windedness it is now grown largely for decorative reasons.
Care: Plant between September and April in ordinary soil. Its fondness for woodland means that it will grow in partial shade. It should be cut down in November. Can be propagated by root division between October and March or in April.
Uses: An infusion of fresh leaves used sparingly for headaches and nerves. It can have an intoxicating effect. Once used as a substitute for tea and in flavouring beer. Decorative in the herb garden.

SYMPHYTUM officinalis
Comfrey

Flowering period: May to August.
Colour: pink or white(flowers).
Height: 60-90 cm.
A tall, wide-growing perennial which is believed to have been brought back by the Crusaders after they learned its value in healing wounds. Coarse, rough, green leaves and flowers growing in spikes. An excellent mulch to place round other herbs and also it helps to break down compost materials.
Care: Because of its height and slightly ungainly appearance it is best grown as a background plant. Sow early in spring thinning to 45 cm. Propagate by root division in spring. Will seed itself.
Uses: A poultice made of roots or leaves is used in healing bruises, swellings, bites and cuts and can also treat rheumatic pains and heal scars. An infusion of leaves helps heal cuts and bites. A decoction of roots eases coughs and as a gargle helps with throat inflammation and bleeding gums. An infusion makes a tonic bath and leaves also make a lotion for dry skin. Add leaves sparingly to salads.

TANACETUM vulgare
Tansy

Flowering period: July to September.
Colour: yellow(flowers).
Height: 60-90 cm.
A pungent perennial herb, native to Europe, with fern-like leaves and golden yellow, button-shaped flowers. It is a plant to be grown with care. Once planted it may never go away, travelling all over by means of its spreading stolons. It was commonly grown in cottage gardens as a herb in medieval Europe and used to make tansy cakes, puddings and other dishes. Especially associated with Easter.
Care: The problem with Tansy is not how to grow it but how to stop it growing. It will grow in profusion from seed or by root division.
Uses: Use leaves to discourage flies and other insects. A mild infusion was once used against threadworm but beware, a strong dose is poisonous. Used on cakes and puddings at Easter to symbolise the Passion.

TARAXACUM officinalis
Dandelion

Flowering period: summer.
Colour: yellow(flowers).
Height: up to 30 cm.
Scorned by many as a weed it is in fact a most useful plant and has the added advantage that it is safe to use in large quantities. A perennial which grows from a taproot it has been used by physicians in ancient times and ever since. All parts of the plant have uses and it is high time its reputation was rescued.
Care: To write about cultivating dandelions is almost to invite ridicule since it grows in profusion but like most herbs it does have favourite conditions. Prefers rich soil and protection in winter. Propagate by division.
Uses: An infusion, or juice, pressed from it is an effective diuretic and good for liver complaints, constipation, insomnia and rheumatism. It is also a good general tonic. Young leaves can be added to salads and an infusion makes a good skin tonic.

THYMUS citriodorus
Lemon Thyme

Flowering period: July to August.
Colour: mauve or pink(flowers).
Height: 20-30 cm.
A perennial evergreen shrub, sweetly scented with lemon and having a strong flavour. Like Rosemary it thrives in the sun. It has a woody stem, small, downy leaves and small clusters of flowers. Once it was said that thyme gave its user courage, strength and even cured shyness.
Care: Sow in early summer in well-drained soil and a sheltered spot. Space plants 30 cm apart. Demon thyme is less hardy than other thymes and may well need winter protection. Propagate by layering from mid-spring to early summer.
Uses: As an ingredient of bouquet garni, for soups and sauces and in meat, poultry and game dishes. Used in a tincture or infusion it aids cough and throat infections and as a tea it helps with flatulence and indigestion. An infusion of leaves or flowers can be used as a skin tonic and facial steam.

THYMUS serpyllum
Wild Thyme

Flowering period: June to August.
Colour: deep red, pink, white(flowers).
Height: 2-6 cm.
A hardy perennial herbaceous plant which exists in many forms but is generally best-suited as a plant for herb lawns. A thick-matting plant it will provide a quick and aromatic carpeting in areas which are not heavily walked. Narrow, grey-green elliptical leaves and flowers which come in rounded terminal clusters.
Care: Plant from October to March. Like most thymes it likes plenty of sun and a dry, well-drained position. Propagate by division in March, August or September. Cut off flower heads to preserve the thick, matted character. Also suits gardens where it will drape itself over rocks and edges.
Uses: Largely ornamental. There are plenty of thymes which can be used for medical, cosmetic or culinary applications. Save this for decoration.

THYMUS vulgare
Common Thyme

Flowering period: July to August.
Colour: mauve(leaves).
Height: up to 45 cm.
Common, or garden, thyme is probably the best known. A perennial, evergreen shrub native to the Mediterranean it has a woody stem, small downy leaves and whorls of flowers which bloom for about a month. Associated with strength and courage and in Middle Ages ladies embroidered sprigs of it into the clothes of knights off to the Crusades. Its leaves contain thymol which is a powerful antiseptic.
Care: It likes a sunny spot in dry, well-drained soil. Sow seeds in spring and thin to 30 cm. Can be propagated by division or from stem cuttings taken in spring.
Uses: Has a powerful aroma and should be used sparingly in cooking. Add to meat, fish and soups. Use in a tincture or infusion for throat infections and as a tea for flatulence and indigestion.

TRIGONELLA foenum-graecum
Fenugreek

Flowering period: late summer.
Colour: yellow.
Height: up to 60 cm.
Grown in Mediterranean countries since ancient times and one of the oldest plants in cultivation. In ancient times it was said to produce a satisfying roundness in ladies' breasts but nowadays its uses are largely culinary. Many people don't like its taste because it reminds them of cheap curry powders. Its leaves can be bitter and so, too, its seeds which should be roasted slowly to develop flavour before being ground. When overheated they turn red and are not good.
Care: Sow just below the surface of soil in drills 25 cm apart. It will grow only in light, lime-rich soil and a very sunny spot.
Uses: As a seasoning in home-made curry powders (to produce the authentic versions). Its activity on the digestive system helps to regulate it and it can also lower blood pressure.

TROPAEOLUM majus
Nasturtium

Flowering period: June to September.
Colour: yellow or orange(flowers).
Height: 30 cm-1 metre.
A round-leaved climbing and trailing annual from Peru but now found all over. Orange or yellow trumpet-like flowers, mid-green leaves and a slight scent. Although called nasturtium it is no relative of watercress (Nasturtium officinalis) but its leaves do have a cress-like flavour.
Care: Sow late in spring to early summer in ordinary garden soil and a sunny spot. It should prosper anywhere if soil is well-drained. It will help to protect neighbouring plants from pests and will grow well in a window box.
Uses: The leaves contain both iron and Vitamin C. A tea made from the flowers, leaves or seeds can be used for chest colds and for respiratory problems. Use young, fresh leaves in salads and sandwiches and pickle the seeds to use as a substitute for capers.

TUSSILAGO farfara
Coltsfoot

Flowering period: March and April.
Colour: yellow(flowers).
Height: 10-40 cm.
A pleasing addition to a herb garden since this creeping perennial is one of the earliest plants to flower and its splendid yellow blooms are welcome after the gloom of winter. Basal, heart-shaped leaves with toothed edges. Leaves have been smoked as tobacco over the ages to cure congestion and asthma.
Care: Not easy to find seeds or plants and you may have to scour the countryside. A plant which should be introduced into your garden carefully anyway because it spreads rapidly.
Uses: Leaves added to a decoction of liquorice root for coughs and colds. A tea from fresh leaves is used to relieve sore throats and congestion. Crushed leaves can be applied to insect bites, sores and burns.

URTICA dioica
Nettle

Flowering period: July to October.
Colour: greenish-white(flowers).
Height: 80-180 cm.
A plant, some say weed, to be grown carefully since it spreads rapidly, but has many uses. When touched its bristly hairs inject an irritant into the skin. Introduced by the Romans who are said to have chastened themselves with nettles to increase circulation and keep warm.
Care: If you have nettles, as most do, to talk about cultivation is irrelevant. If not introduce into your garden with great care and in a remote, perhaps wild, spot. Try planting just a few roots found wild and bury roofing slates around them to stop them growing.
Uses: Fresh juice stimulates digestion and stems internal bleeding including excessive menstrual flow. Reduces susceptibility to rheumatism and migraine and applied externally is used for chilblains. Makes a face pack for dry skin.

VALERIANA officinalis
Valerian

Flowering period: July to August.
Colour: pink or white(flowers).
Height: up to 1 metre.
A perennial plant with short, straggly roots which contain a volatile oil. When dried the roots give off an offensive odour which accounts for its nickname 'phew'. Rats love the plant and rumour has it that the Pied Piper of Hamlin was no magician merely an expert herbalist who knew the power of Valerian. Seldom grown these days but a small clump, tended to stop it spreading, will find some medical use.
Care: Sow in spring under glass and plant into damp but well-drained soil in a sunny spot. Valerian is slow to cultivate so a quicker method would be root division in spring or autumn.
Uses: Grown for its roots which, in a decoction, relieve tension, headache and other nervous disorders. Anglo-Saxons used the leaves as a salad herb.

VERBASCUM thapsus
Mullein

Flowering period: June to August.
Colour: yellow(flowers).
Height: up to 90 cm.
A stately perennial which will stand out in your herb garden. Thick, white foliage, sturdy stems and yellow flowers borne in 30-45 cm long spikes make it a very striking plant. Similarities with a torch are not merely coincidental because for many years it was dipped in wax and used in that fashion. During its first year the large rosettes are formed and it cannot be relied upon to transplant well.
Care: Likes ordinary, well-drained soil in full sun. Plant in October, March or April. Sow seeds during April in seed compost and place in a cold frame. Prick out to 15 cm and grow on, planting seedlings direct into the flowering site in September.
Uses: For coughs – especially long hacking coughs – drink a tea made from the flowers.

VERBENA officinalis
Vervain

Flowering period: July to September.
Colour: lilac(flowers).
Height: 70-80 cm.
A perennial plant with spear-shaped leaves and small flowers carried on long stems. In ancient Persia the plant was reputed to have magical, medicinal and culinary uses. Hippocrates wrote glowingly about it and the Druids used it to cure the plague. In Tudor times it was used as an aphrodisiac.
Care: Grow in fertile soil in a sunny, open spot. Sow seeds under glass in January or March barely covering with compost and at a temperature of 18-21C (64-70F). Not all seeds will germinate and it may take 3-4 weeks. Prick out into boxes and harden off before planting out in May.
Uses: The leaves can be used in an infusion which treats urinary problems.

VINCA minor
Lesser Periwinkle

Flowering period: March to July.
Colour: blue(flowers).
Height: 5-10 cm.
An evergreen, mat-forming shrub whose use is largely decorative. It forms an attractive ground-cover in an herbaceous border or rock garden. The leaves are elliptic and lance-shaped and a glossy green colour. The blue flowers may continue as late as October.
Care: It should be grown in a partially-shaded position in any ordinary soil which is well-drained. Sow seeds in boxes of compost in March at a temperature of 15-18C (59-64F). Prick out into boxes and when large enough into 10 cm pots of compost. To encourage growth pinch out the tips. Plant out in May or June. Can be propagated by cuttings taken in March or by division at any time between September and April.
Uses: Largely ornamental.

VIOLA odorata
Sweet Violet

Flowering period: February to April.
Colour: purple or white(flowers).
Height: 10-15 cm.
A sweet-scented herbaceous perennial known since ancient times and a herb regarded as a symbol of constancy which has given it a reputation as one of the most romantic plants. Napoleon is said to have given sweet violets to Josephine on each wedding anniversary and, when banished, he is said to have promised to return with violets in the spring. It forms thick tufts of rhizomes and spreads by runners. It has heart-shaped, mid to dark-green leaves.
Care: Plant in September, October, March or April in well-drained soil and in sun or partial shade. Propagate by cuttings $1/2$-1 cm long taken from non-flowering base shoots in July and placed in a mixture of equal parts sand and peat. Pot on and plant out between September and March.
Uses: Preserve flowers in sugar as crystallized violets and use flowers and leaves as decoration.

VISCUM album
Mistletoe

Flowering period: February to April.
Colour: yellowish green(flowers).
Height: 30-90 cm.
A parasitic hardy evergreen shrub which grows on a variety of trees, though not oaks or conifers. Native to Europe and Asia it bears yellowish green leaves in alternate pairs on forking twigs which form a globular white fruit on the female plant only. Flowers form in clusters from February to April. The almost translucent white fruits which appear from September to January on the female plant contain a sticky pulp.
Care: Can be propagated in February or March by pressing the ripe berries inside the bark crevices or on the underside of a branch. The seeds may well take as much as two or three months to germinate and they will not bear fruit for up to seven years.
Uses: Mistletoe has been the symbol of love and affection for centuries and is very popular as a decoration at Christmas. Beware, the berries are poisonous.

INDEX OF USES

INDEX OF USES

FIRMS AND NURSERIES

Avon: ★ Culpeper the Herbalist, 28 Milsom Street, Bath.

Berkshire: ★ Hollington Nurseries Ltd., Woolton Hill, Newbury.

Breconshire: ★ Senni Valley Herb Farm, Senni, Sennybridge.

Birmingham: ★ Midland Herbs and Spices, 228 Warwick Road, Greet, Birmingham.

Buckinghamshire: ★ Lathbury Park Herb Gardens, Newport Pagnell.

Cambridgeshire: ★ Culpeper the Herbalist, 25 Lion Yard, Cambridge ★ Nornea Herb Farms Ltd., Nornea, Ely ★ Herbs From the Hoo, 46 Church Street, Buckden, Huntingdon.

Cornwall: ★ Polsue Cottage Herbs, Ruan High Lanes, Truro.

Dorset: ★ Arne Farm, Arne, Wareham ★ Cranborne Garden Centre, Cranborne, Wimborne.

Essex: ★ Herbs in Stock, Whites Hill, Stock, Ingatestone.

Hampshire: ★ A. Dorsett, The Cottage, Dogmersfield Park, Dogmersfield, Nr Fleet ★ Sutton manor Herb Farm, Sutton Scotney, Winchester.

Hertfordshire: Hatfield House, Hatfield.

Herefordshire: ★ Hereford Herbs, Remenham House, Ocle Pychard ★ Stoke Lacey Herb Garden, Nr. Bromyard.

Kent: ★ Iden Croft Nurseries and Herb Farm, Frittenden Road, Staplehurst ★ Old Rectory Herb Farm, Ightham, Nr Sevenoaks ★ Wells and Winter Ltd., Mereworth, Maidstone.

London: ★ Culpeper the Herbalist, The Market, Covent Garden.

Norfolk: ★ Norfolk Lavender Ltd., Caley Mill, Heacham, King's Lynn ★ Daphne Fiske, 2 Station Road, Brundall.

Oxfordshire: ★ Culpeper the Herbalist, 7 New Inn Hall Street.

Shropshire: ★ Laundry Farm Herbs, Nescliffe ★ Oak Cottage Herb Farm, Nescliffe ★ Valeswood, Little Ness, Shrewsbury.

Somerset: ★ Bristol Botanic Products, Church Lane, Bristol 8.

Suffolk: ★ Hofels Pure Foods Ltd., Woolpit, Bury St. Edmonds ★ Honeyrose Products Ltd., PO Box 4, Creeting Road, Stowmarket ★ Netherfield Herbs, 37 Nether Street, Rougham ★ Suffolk Herbs, Sawyers Farm, Little Cornard, Sudbury – Thornham Herbs, The Walled Garden, Thornham Magne, Eye.

Surrey: ★ The Hedgerow Centre, Nr Farnham ★ Culpeper the Herbalist, 10 Swan Lane, Guildford ★ Hulbrook House, Shamley Green, Nr Guildford ★ Lomond, Horsehill, Hookwood, Horley.

Sussex: ★ Binstead Herbs, Binstead, Arundel ★ Culpeper the Herbalist, 12d Meeting House Lane, Brighton ★ Tidebrook Manor Farm, Wadhurst.

Warwickshire: ★ Lighthorne Associates Ltd., Lighthorne Rough, Moreton Morrell.

Wiltshire: ★ Culpeper the Herbalist, 33 High Street, Salisbury.

Yorkshire: ★ The Herb Centre. Middleton Tyas, Richmond.

INDEX OF PLANT NAMES

INDEX OF PLANT NAMES